RHYTHM OF LIFE

SERIES EDITOR: BISHOP GRAHAM CHADWICK

A CONDITION OF COMPLETE SIMPLICITY

*Franciscan wisdom
for today's world*

ROWAN CLARE WILLIAMS

CANTERBURY
PRESS

Norwich

First published in 2003 by the Canterbury Press Norwich
(a publishing imprint of Hymns Ancient & Modern Limited,
a registered charity)
St Mary's Works, St Mary's Plain,
Norwich, Norfolk, NR3 3BH

www.scm-canterburypress.co.uk

British Library Cataloguing in Publication data

A catalogue record for this book is available
from the British Library

ISBN 1-85311-538-X

Typeset by Regent Typesetting, London
Printed and bound by
Bookmarque, Croydon, Surrey

A Condition of Complete Simplicity

Rowan Clare Williams was for seven years a member of the Community of St Francis, an Anglican religious order. She is currently training for the Anglican priesthood at Westcott House, Cambridge.

Other titles in the *Rhythm of Life* series

THE BOOK OF CREATION
– the practice of Celtic spirituality
Philip Newell

CALLED TO BE ANGELS
– an introduction to Anglo-Saxon spirituality
Douglas Dales

ETERNITY NOW
– an introduction to Orthodox spirituality
Mother Thekla

THE FIRE OF LOVE
– praying with Thérèse of Lisieux
James McCaffrey

LIVING WITH CONTRADICTION
– an introduction to Benedictine spirituality
Esther de Waal

TO LIVE IS TO PRAY
– an introduction to Carmelite spirituality
Elizabeth Ruth Obbard

THE WAY OF ECSTASY
– praying with Teresa of Avila
Peter Tyler

Forthcoming

COMPANIONS OF CHRIST
– Ignation spirituality for everyday living
Margaret Silf

In memory of Violet Williams
1911–2000

Many waters cannot quench love,
neither can the floods drown it.

(Song of Songs 8:7)

Contents

Acknowledgements

I would like to thank the sisters and brothers of the three orders of the Society of Saint Francis. Especial thanks are due to Angelo SSF and Rose CSF for permission to quote from their respective articles in *Franciscan* magazine, to Helen Julian CSF for her unfailing support during the writing of the book, and to Professor John Sloboda and the Revd Jack McDonald for their comments on the text.

© The European Province of the Society of Saint Francis for material from *The Principles* and *The Daily Office SSF*.

The Scripture quotations contained herein are from The New Revised Standard version of the Bible, Anglicized Edition, © 1989, 1995 by the Division of Christian Education of the National Council of the Churches of Christ in the United States of America, and are used by permission. No rights reserved.

© New City Press, New York, for permission to reproduce material from *Francis of Assisi: Early Documents*, vols 1–3, edited by Regis J. Armstrong, J. A. Wayne Hellmann and William J. Short.

Series Introduction

*'Wisdom is to discern the true rhythm of things:
joy is to move, to dance to that rhythm.'*

This series of books on various traditions of Christian
spirituality is intended as an introduction for beginners
on the journey of faith. It might help us discover a truer
rhythm as something of the experience of those who
follow any particular tradition resonates with our own.

Too much can be made of the distinctions between the
different expressions of Christian spirituality. They all
derive from the experience of what God has done and is
doing in us and among us. While emphases differ, their
validity is their congruence with the good news of Jesus
Christ in the scriptures. As the various instruments in an
orchestra make their special contribution to the sym-
phony, so we delight in the extra dimension that each
tradition brings to the living out of the Christian faith.

The present wide interest in spirituality seems to indicate that, in the midst of all the current uncertainties that
we meet in contemporary life, despite its relative comfort
and technological advance, there is felt a need to recon-
nect with our spiritual roots and find a deeper purpose
for living.

Each volume offers an introduction to the essential elements of the particular spiritual tradition and practical guidance for shaping our everyday lives according to its teaching and wisdom. It is an exploration into the way that spiritual practice can affect our lifestyle, work, relationships, our view of creation, patterns of prayer and worship, and responsibilities in the wider world.

Many books, of course, have been written in all of these areas and in each tradition classic commentaries are available which can never be surpassed. The aim of this series is to meet the needs of those searching for or beginning to explore the journey inward into their inmost being and outward to relationship with people and the whole of creation.

St Francis can be of special help in our attitude to creation, in our relationship with people and in many other ways. His life of contemplation and action is a signpost for all Christians at all times, not least our own. As the author of this book points out, the keynotes of Franciscan spirituality are humility, love and joy. They were lived out in times of violence, greed and interfaith conflict.

As we see the values of the upside-down kingdom of God lived out by Francis, we can be helped to deal radically with the problems of today. They can throw light on questions of suffering, commercialism, conservation of the environment and violence. Franciscan spirituality has much to tell us about peacemaking and attitudes to the disadvantaged and to the stranger in our midst.

The author's own experience as a Franciscan sister particularly in the inner city lends authenticity to all that she writes.

Bishop Graham Chadwick
Sarum College
March 2003

Introduction

If there is one symbol that can sum up contemporary
Western culture, it is probably the mobile phone. Anyone
who has ever sat next to a mobile user on a train has
received the clear message that this is a symbol of status,
busyness, maybe even of arrogance: 'I'm important and
I'm going to make sure you know I'm here.' It's also a
reminder of our global perspective – practically nowhere
now is unreachable – and the pressure on our time.
No time, it seems, can be wasted in just being – *doing*
and *working* are the main justifications for existing. The
pace of modern life feels unstoppable. Life, we're led to
believe, has to be loud, fast, commercial, materialist and
obsessed with achievement. Nothing else counts. The
insistent beep of the mobile has become as much part of
the fabric of our lives as the values it represents.

Mobiles also speak powerfully of another aspect of
contemporary life: our desperate need for recognition
and connection, to be heard and seen for who we really
are, if only we can work out who that is. Perhaps they
actually speak of insecurity, rather than arrogance.
'*Please* acknowledge me,' they trill. 'I matter. I'm here.
Notice me!' They speak across a hungry void, trying to
communicate, filling the emptiness with sound. Perhaps

each individual conversation signifies little except to those most immediately involved, but each one is a small symbol of the universal human drive to make some kind of impact on the world, to communicate something unique, and to be heard.

The events of Tuesday 11 September, 2001, burned themselves into our consciousness in an unprecedented way. That day, too, mobile phones acquired yet another significance. There were a number of stories of people who found themselves on the hijacked planes or in the World Trade Centre, using their mobiles to say to family and friends: 'I want you to know I love you before I die.' Archbishop Rowan Williams, in his book of reflections on the events of that day, rightly points out the dangers of making cheap theological points out of people's suffering. Not everyone's last thoughts would have been of love – there must also have been fear, hatred, anger.[1] Yet, as he also acknowledges, there *was* a poignancy in the way many people needed to reach out to each other in those last moments, to communicate something of real and lasting importance, to reassert their sense of interconnection and belonging. When you are about to die, money and power lose all meaning. They cannot define who you are as a person. So the mobiles still said 'I'm important, I'm here', but we suddenly heard them in a new way.

Any discussion of the nature of the modern world now has to take into account the reality of global terrorism. It has become increasingly clear that there is no immunity from the effects of terror: contrary to what the affluent West may once have wanted to imagine, it is no longer something which only happens to other people in inaccessible parts of the world. Recent rhetoric about a 'war on terror' highlights the larger-scale battle for moral and ideological supremacy which has shaped Western cultural identity in the global era. In a climate of general insecurity about what Western culture actually is, that identity has been easier to describe negatively than positively: we may not be too clear about who 'we' are, but we know that we are not 'them'. This defensive mentality contributes largely to the continuing East–West standoff. Such an atmosphere breeds mutual suspicion, confusion and disinformation over core values. It does not encourage the possibility of finding an adequate response to terrorism or to the conditions which have caused it to flourish. Instead, what is desperately needed, if paranoia and hysteria are not to triumph, is a more sustained attempt to understand those it would be easier to demonize as 'not like us'. Such attempts to *understand* the roots of terror need not be seen as condoning evil. A sensible and mature approach to the manifestation of evil is very necessary in every culture – perhaps even more so in a culture which has become uncomfortable with conventional religious language and the idea that it might have something to say to us.

Franciscan spirituality is perhaps uniquely placed to grapple with these dominant issues for our culture. In particular, it presents an important challenge to the individualism which also characterizes contemporary culture, and which has contributed to the harmful separation between 'them' and 'us'. The phenomenon of globalism, for example, is not necessarily a bad thing. It does not have to mean a characterless homogeneity, or the automatic subsuming of the small by the rich and powerful. A positive perspective on globalism does not shrink the world but opens it up. With access to more information about the world and its people comes more awareness of what life is like for those people; in that awareness is found the possibility of learning how to tolerate difference for the greater good.

Underlying this increased sense of global citizenship is a sense of connectedness which simply was not available to us before. In this light, the Franciscan emphasis on community is more than a response to the need to be recognized and noticed; it is a living out of the universal worth of each person. Ironically, considering the anti-Islamic dogma which characterized Francis' time as it does our own, this vision of universal and mutual concern for human welfare is oddly similar to the Muslim concept of the *umma*. Human beings drastically need a way of living faith with integrity which does not require the destruction of those who think differently. To be able to see another, however ostensibly different, as a fellow human being made in the image of God, is a significant step towards peace. The moment when 'them' becomes 'us' is a profound moment of conversion.

As we shall explore in later chapters, the life of St Francis was a *series* of conversion moments, each one a staging post on a continuing journey deeper and deeper into union with Christ. In one typically dramatic and literal gesture, Francis publicly cast off everything his earthly father had ever given him – home, name, security, wealth, clothing – to become utterly dependent on God. Instead of an earthly family, Francis came to recognize all creatures as his brothers and sisters, seeing and revering in them something of the image of the Creator. Above all, he wanted to show the reality of his conversion by embracing a whole new way of living – and he did so to such effect that the world around him began to question its former values, and to explore afresh what it might mean to live for Christ alone.

Francis is a joyful figure. His life was characterized by celebration, laughter and a deep love of the whole creation. The very attractiveness of the image can often encourage a distorted picture ('St Francis of Assisi? Isn't he the saint who liked animals?'). If that had been all, he would have nothing of worth to say to our current situation. Popular piety often depicts him as a cosy little pastel saint surrounded by birds. To see him in that light, however, trivializes his true impact. For Francis was, and is, *not* just a voice only for the good times of fun and celebration. His Christian discipleship was set firmly in the way of the cross. The process of his own conversion led him to preach in no uncertain terms of the importance of repentance, of dying in order to live.

There can be no easy path to resurrection. If there is any meaning to be found in pain and death, it is found *in* and *through* it, not in spite of it. Franciscan spirituality does not ignore the dark side of life. Instead, it seeks to find traces of the divine in everything, no matter how prosaic or painful, in order to help us keep our hearts and minds open to the promise of resurrection. There is no ideal world in which to undertake our search for God. We have only the broken, embattled world in which we already live – and in which God's love is already abundantly at work, if only we could see it.

If we are to understand Francis' importance as a sign-post for our contemporary questioning, we will need to re-examine some of the popular myths about him. To do so need not destroy the true core of his attraction. Instead, the fire of his conversion can inspire and set us alight to find God at work in our own time. As a youth, Francis sought glamour and fame through service as a knight. Choosing instead to serve his Master in heaven, his hunger for fame and glory was transformed into a lasting joy in simplicity. So Francis can now prompt us to rediscover our own true desire. He accompanies us as we hunt for meaning and for God in the 'real world' we live in. He can lead us to do battle with false priorities, both in ourselves and in our culture. The world needs to hear Francis' message again – perhaps more than ever as we come to terms with the fragility of existing political, economic and religious structures. His ministry of peace-making and reconciliation ('taming' hungry wolves, speaking with the Muslim Sultan at the time of the Fifth Crusade) has an obvious, urgent, contemporary relevance. But his insistence on a literal following of Christ reminds us how much it can cost to choose the way of peace in any age.

Franciscan spirituality is often described as very down-to-earth. It does not shrink from encountering reality head on: but it always tries to do so with love. The world we now live in is as divided, unjust and violent as was Francis' own. Yet in that same world he saw endless causes for hope, for rejoicing, as he saw Christ's presence mirrored in every creature he encountered. So there is no excuse for giving up on this twenty-first-century world, for retiring into cynicism or despair at our apparent failure to progress. People today need to know they are lovable and valuable as much now as they ever did – perhaps even more so. They need hope. Whether or not they adhere to a religious faith, people still need to hear and understand the promise of resurrection – that even after death and destruction, life can still flourish.

The world as we know it has not been destroyed by terrorism. The same apparently trivial mobile conversations still go on, as they always did – but underneath their irritating electronic beeping, it is perhaps easier than before to discern the voices asking '*Who am I? What is my place in this world? If our hold on life is so fragile, how can I ever again believe that I really matter?*' Rooted in life as it truly is, able to spot traces of God at work in every human event from birth to death, Franciscan spirituality offers the possibility of a positive response to such essential questions.

Universal Vocation

Nearly eight hundred years after Francis' death, there are millions of people across the world who try to represent the values and challenges of that little poor man in the way they live their daily lives. Franciscans live out in microcosm the vocation of *all* Christians – to love and to be present to a world which too often stifles the voices of the poor and insignificant. We know the importance of *being there* with those who hurt, reflecting Christ by continuing to love despite the cost, and by daring to hang on to our humanity even when reality starts to bite. Franciscans are called to live as an incarnational presence in the world. Anyone who walks in the footsteps of Francis is led right into the middle of all the mess caused by evil and suffering. He refused to shy away from painful confrontations with reality, but insisted that God's voice can and must be heard in every situation. Only by following his example can we stand any chance in our own time of getting across the vital message that we are all God's people, and God does not leave us to hurt alone. It is a risky vocation, but one essential for the survival of our world. For it is into the *whole* range of human experience, not just into the easily sanitized parts, that God comes in the shape of Christ.

Perhaps the costliest part of a Franciscan vocation is to recognize that it is not only the victims but also the perpetrators of violence and terror who are our brothers and sisters. Demonizing those who do terrible things cannot help. It is perhaps only by taking the risk of acknowledging their humanity as of equal validity with our own, that we can hope to make the voice of love and peace heard above the screams of hatred and vengeance. Each one of us needs to make that journey of acknowledgement, to recognize that we are already involved, and we cannot pretend otherwise. We too have to recognize our potential to do evil as well as good. Whether in the World Trade Centre, the mountains of Afghanistan or the streets of Omagh, in Israel or Palestine, in Auschwitz, in Iraq or Sierra Leone or Sudan or Vietnam, it is our brothers and sisters who have been and are being killed. And those who kill are human like other humans: human, that is, exactly like us.

If there is any hope of bringing lasting good out of the evils of terrorism, war and hatred, we need to hear the challenge of prophets like Francis, who confront our values but affirm our humanity in the face of what we know of its destructive potential. We need to reflect on who we are and the values we *really* wish to promote in the world – and then get on with living them. By exploring what it means to walk in the way of St Francis in our world today, I wonder if we might not begin to find seeds of hope blossoming even out of the most appalling destruction.

It may seem an obscenity even to try to find anything resembling Good News as we struggle to come to terms with a world where terrorism is a commonplace means of communication. However, if we can continue to believe in a God who is present in some way in *every* human experience, we may begin to find a way forward, however halting and inadequate it seems. Over and over again we are called to contemplate the mystery that even in the worst times, when Easter is unimaginably far away, God is nevertheless right there at work. God does not remain safely on the outside looking on at our suffering, but is deeply, intimately, involved with it. We do not like reminders of our vulnerability and neediness. But in the Incarnation, God deliberately takes our vulnerable humanity and lives it fully, absolutely – messiness, failure, death and all.

The keynotes of Franciscan spirituality are humility, love and joy. For Francis, and for those who seek to walk in his way, they are the fruits of that continuing process of conversion which begins with Jesus' call to 'come, follow me'.[2] They allow us to examine new ways of engaging with the world. The attempt to live with others in humility, love and joy opens up the possibility of finding and reflecting Christ anywhere we happen to be; the more broken and damaged our world appears, the more it needs to see humility, love and joy in action.

Saints are ordinary people who find in themselves the resources to do extraordinary things. Francis' way of life was devastatingly simple. He witnessed to a manner of living which is rooted in dependence on God, rather than on any power or status we may have accumulated for ourselves. Everything we have has been given to us, and to come with honesty before God we need to start, as Francis did, with nothing. God looks with love on our frailties and hesitations, and still he invites us: 'Come, follow me'.

Modern life, at least in the affluent West, offers a bewildering range of choices and possibilities. We are uncertain what to choose. How will we know if we have made the right choice? Competing values clamour for our attention until we are almost paralysed by indecision. We yearn for simplicity. But to begin again with nothing feels very exposed. We are afraid of our vulnerability. A life of humility, love and joy in the pattern of St Francis offers a strange freedom, but one so different from what we are used to that we scarcely recognize what it has to offer.

Even if we can bear to risk it, the way ahead is by no means easy. The complex questions of existence do not simply melt away. Yet Francis' life, shorn of choice, free from all encumbrances, but radiantly in love with God, offers a hopeful model for life in harmony with the true ground of our being:

> A condition of complete simplicity
> (Costing not less than everything)
> And all shall be well and
> All manner of thing shall be well.[3]

Part One
Humility

Humility is the recognition of the truth about God and ourselves, the recognition of our own insufficiency and dependence, seeing that we have nothing that we have not received.

(*The Principles of the First Order of the Society of Saint Francis*, Day 25)

I

Life and Context

Among all the other gifts which we have received and continue to receive daily from our benefactor, the Father of mercies, and for which we must express the deepest thanks to our glorious God, our vocation is a great gift.

(*The Testament of St Clare*)[1]

Francis has become one of the best-known and best-loved saints of recent times. It is odd to think that, after his intense popularity in his own time and immediately after his death, he was little known or studied until the end of the nineteenth century. He didn't write all that much himself, but after he was canonized almost immediately after his death, several Lives of St Francis were written. Some were by people who had actually known him, often early brothers of the order, so his story as told by them does have an immediacy recognizable from the Gospels. The first 'modern' attempt at a scholarly Life of St Francis was published in 1894 by the French author Paul Sabatier, and the thirst for Franciscan spirituality has hardly slackened since.

The Challenge of St Francis

So who *was* St Francis, and what does he have to say to

us today, nearly 800 years after his death? He remains a hugely charismatic figure, and his way to God attracts many people through its sincerity and wholeheartedness. Conventional images of Francis conjure up a dreamy-faced young man in a brown habit, surrounded by birds and animals. He is often made to appear sweet and unthreatening, even whimsical. Yet this image of him is seriously misleading. It is unlikely that such a person could have a lasting impact over eight centuries; still less that he could have any valid message for a cynical and questioning generation like our own. Perhaps the animal-lover persona has been imposed on Francis in order to soften the real bite of his message for today – to keep him 'safe' so that we do not have to take him seriously? We do not want to be reminded that gospel living, if it is done wholeheartedly, is anything but safe. Over-emphasizing the cute, animal-loving Francis enables us to miss the point – that following Christ is a dangerous vocation. Complete simplicity has its cost.

Francis has much more to offer us. His way of being in the world has a great deal of significance for our behaviour and attitudes. It is not because he skips around facilely chanting 'hullo trees hullo sky' like an adult fotherington-tomas[2] that Francis has become the patron saint of nature and ecology! Instead, much more demandingly, he points to a new way of living as a citizen of the world. Not just other human beings but *all* creatures, from the elements to the insects, are our partners in a song of praise to God who created all of us for relationship and co-existence. Psychology has made us much more aware of how self-centred we are. But embarking on the Franciscan way demands that we question ourselves profoundly. What is at the heart of my life? Does my knowledge of myself, and of God, lead me into relationship with others as they really are, or only as they are of use to me?

If we take on Francis' challenge, we will be required to relinquish our sense of control. There is no room here for a sense of superiority about our place in the created order. We do not have the right to exploit other creatures for our own satisfaction, or to satisfy our own perceptions of what we need. In Francis' vision, we have no right of power or dominion over our environment, but are required to work *with* it. Most vitally of all, we are called to recognize the hand of God at work in our lives, and in the lives of all the other creatures who share our space. God is at the centre of this equation. A right relationship with each creature involves learning to know it as its Creator intended it to be known; understanding the purpose of its existence, enabling it to fulfil whatever potential it has to reflect that Creator back to other creatures.

Such a view was revolutionary in Francis' time, and little, essentially, has changed; although we have made great advances in scientific understanding, our view of ourselves as the real masters of the universe has done untold damage to our environment. So Francis' sermons to the birds and the animals become a contemporary challenge to all who are capable of understanding. We desperately need to rediscover the humility that characterizes Francis' whole approach to his world. And we also need to rediscover God at the centre of life.

A Way of Commitment

Christians do not have a monopoly on the desire to live well and fulfil our human potential. The Church, at least in the affluent West, has to adjust to the fact that it has lost much of its former power to influence what people believe or how they behave. Moreover, those of us who call ourselves Christian have to face the fact that it is now *our* beliefs that are counter-cultural, marginalized, irrelevant to the mainstream culture in which we live. Here too, Francis may be able to indicate a way forward. Although he was always loyal to the institutional Church, that very loyalty led Francis to question the institution from the inside, in a way that a mere interested observer could not have done. Slavish obedience to an institution – 'my Church, right or wrong' – would not have led Francis or his soul-mate St Clare to insist on the adoption of their respective Rules against the wisdom of the hierarchy. And an institution which stifled opposition by insisting on slavish obedience could not have allowed itself to be won over by their vision, or their persistence. It is not for nothing that *obedience* has its root in the Latin *audire*, to hear. Listening to each other is essential for growth in any relationship. Francis and Clare found the root of their vocation was in obedient, attentive listening to God.

Such concepts may seem alien to a world which has grown used to the rational as the only approach. Insistence on a loving God can seem impossibly naive when faced with disaster. Religion itself is discredited by the devastation wreaked by fundamentalists of every creed. However, whether or not there is any room in our personal philosophy for a God, we will all need at some stage to question the values that shape our lives. What truly lies at the heart of our life defines who we are. Francis' life shows the possibility of living with complete consistency.

Much anxiety is expressed nowadays about our apparent fear of lasting commitments. This is demonstrated, or so the argument goes, by shifts in attitude to relationships, to institutions, or indeed to the concept that *any* hard and fast rules can apply to the way we live. It is often assumed that this fear is especially prevalent among younger people. In my own experience, however, it has little to do with being *incapable* of commitment. It is not that my generation is any less willing to follow our values than those who came before us. It is, rather, that we take commitment extremely seriously, and we are only too aware of the pain that can be caused when it breaks down. In the affluent West, at least, we are presented with such a range of choices that we are paralysed by the fear of choosing wrongly and losing everything which gave our lives meaning. Simplicity is paradoxically seductive to people who are continually being bombarded with 'lifestyle choices'. Having *no* choice rescues us from the anxiety of choosing from among a barrage of options. Discovering our utter dependence on God sets us free to be ourselves.

Francis' gift is to make such absolute commitment seem attractive to the ordinary person. He shows that it is possible to give up everything one has been taught to value, and yet remain totally oneself. Francis himself emerged from this process as someone very human and certainly fallible, yet uncompromised in his attempt to live his faith to the full. Living without props, with no protection and no evasion, seems suddenly possible for the rest of us.

The way of Francis is intensely earthy and real, full of joy and celebration of life as it *is*, and eager to improve what it *could be*. A living faith needs to equip us for real life. To walk in the way of Francis gives us the opportunity not to escape the painful parts, nor yet to wallow in suffering when it comes to us, but to try to integrate it and find whatever meaning there may be in it. As we struggle with the hard questions of human existence, Francis is alongside, offering us as a model his own unchanging priority: 'My God and my all.'

The figure and message of Francis appeal across religions, as well as to many of those who try to live with integrity and justice but espouse no formal religious faith. His journeys to Africa to meet and discuss faith with representatives of Islam establish him as an important figure in the history of peaceful interfaith dialogue. However, it is impossible to speak of following Francis in any truly meaningful way without understanding that for him, to live was to follow Christ. Few saints have demonstrated more graphically or literally what it means to do so. Throughout his life, Francis sought with increasing fervour to become united with the person, life and passion of Jesus. Two years before his death, he received a tangible sign of the reality of that developing union – the stigmata, the wounds of Christ, in his hands and feet and side. Paul's statement, 'It is no longer I who live, but Christ who lives in me',[3] could have been the blueprint for Francis' own discipleship.

The way of Francis is, or should be, the way of Christ. The point of exploring Franciscan spirituality (a term of which Francis would certainly not have approved) is therefore not to focus on Francis himself, but to use him as a lens to God. However, in order to understand Francis' particular impact, or his potential as a guide for our own pattern of discipleship, we do need to know something of his history.

Background

Giovanni Bernardone was born in the Italian town of Assisi, probably in 1181 or 1182. His father, Pietro Bernardone, was a cloth merchant who traded with France, and his mother, Pica, was a Frenchwoman. So Giovanni became known as 'Francesco', the little French one, which translates into English as Francis. He was brought up according to the norms for a wealthy mercantile family of the time. Money was just coming into its own after the age of barter, and the merchant class was beginning to find itself a considerable political and social force. Francis, therefore, grew up as a member of a family of consequence. His early biographers hint that he was overindulged, used to the best of everything. It is clear that as a young man he was something of a leader on the social 'scene' in Assisi, with a large gang of friends and an appetite for parties and music. The *Life of Saint Francis* by Thomas of Celano makes much of Francis' dissolute youth, in order to point up the extent to which his life was changed by direct encounter with God: '[Francis] miserably wasted and squandered his time almost up to the twenty-fifth year of his life. Maliciously advancing beyond all of his peers in vanities, he proved himself a more excessive inciter of evil and a more zealous imitator of foolishness.'[4]

Conversion Experiences

Like most Christians who take their faith seriously, Francis underwent not one single conversion but a *series* of conversion experiences. For him there was not just one blinding flash, but a revelation of different layers of truth and conviction. A number of different visionary experiences over a period of years pushed him deeper and deeper into the search for God. The exact chronology of these experiences is difficult to determine, but it is certain that their cumulative effect was to change Francis' life for ever. His sense of mission developed gradually as each was absorbed into the fabric of his relationship with God.

Like Ignatius of Loyola, Francis' first urge to change direction came through an episode of illness and dependence. He had taken the path of many young men of his class by seeking fame and fortune in a military campaign: Italy at that time was divided into separate city states, and Francis had joined in the battle between Assisi and Perugia, only to be wounded and captured. During that period of imprisonment, he began to experience unease and dissatisfaction with the direction his life was taking. It was not, yet, enough to provoke him to radical change, but it was the first in a series of warning bells which it eventually became impossible to ignore. Perhaps this experience of enforced simplicity, having nothing which his captors did not choose to give him, was his first indicator of the possibilities of a life of dependence on a generous God.

After a year in prison in Perugia, Francis was ransomed by his father and went home, first to convalesce and then to work in the family cloth business. It is not uncommon that families who have paid a ransom to free one of their members from imprisonment come, consciously or otherwise, to feel that they have in some way bought the person's loyalty. This could only have served to emphasize the growing clash of values between Francis and his father. Francis was not to be bought. Ties of commerce, and even ties of affection, had to give way to the call of God, which was becoming too compelling to withstand.

As Francis' health improved, questions again began to surface about how he might best serve God. Celano remarks that Francis was still trying to 'avoid the divine grasp',[5] a sensation surely familiar to anyone who has struggled with the nature of vocation. Francis' initial response was to try the life of chivalry again, intending to join a campaign to Apulia, in the south of the country. One night he dreamed of a house full of soldiers' equipment, and assumed that this meant he would succeed in his quest for military honours. Instead, however, it became clear to him that this was not what the dream really meant. He was not to go to Apulia after all, but God would arm him instead for the struggle which

would concern him most deeply for the rest of his life –
his own battle to do the will of God, whatever the cost.

Francis then withdrew into a time of intense prayer
and meditation. It is during this period that the tension
between activity and contemplation in the Franciscan
tradition first becomes apparent. On the one hand,
Francis was burning to *do* something to indicate his
eagerness to serve God in whatever capacity he was
called to; on the other, he seems always to have known
that only long periods of prayer and solitude would
produce the answers on which he was to act.

At this time, Francis was gripped by a growing conviction that in order to serve God fully, he would have to
become poor. If there was a Damascus road for Francis,
it was one of the roads outside Assisi where, out riding
one day, he encountered a leper. Lepers, of course, were
outcasts from society; they could not live inside the town
walls but had to scratch an existence as best they could
from begging. Francis the rich man's son found them
physically repulsive to the point of nausea. The mountain road did not offer any possibility of escape from this
direct encounter. He passed the leper, but then felt
impelled to dismount from his horse, approach the man,
embrace and kiss him. Some versions of the story under-
line the moral by claiming that when Francis looked
back down the road after this meeting, there was no sign
of the leper, despite the lack of side-roads. In any case, it
struck Francis powerfully that in touching the leper, he
was in fact embracing Christ. From that day onwards he
had a special concern for lepers, whom he referred to as
'Christian brothers'.[6] Further, he saw in this man who

had no possessions, status or security a mirror for his own way of service to God. Becoming a friend and brother of lepers, whether literally affected by leprosy or unwelcome to mainstream society for other reasons, put Francis himself firmly on the margins – but Franciscan living recognizes that society's margins may well be God's centre.

Such a seismic shift in values did not go down well with Francis' family. His former friends and associates found it embarrassing to see the well-born, stylish Francis in the company of 'non-people'. There was widespread mockery, and accusations of insanity. The final, decisive break with the past came when Francis went to pray in the dilapidated old church of San Damiano. An old crucifix hung there, and Francis had spent some hours in contemplation before it when he thought he heard Jesus speaking to him from the cross: 'Francis, go and rebuild my church, which as you see is falling down.' Typically impetuous, he began to gather stones to rebuild San Damiano, which later became the home of the first Franciscan women, St Clare and her Poor Ladies. Francis then travelled to Foligno, a few kilometres from Assisi, to sell some of his father's cloth. Instead of returning home with the money, he gave it to the priest at San Damiano, although this 'gift' was not accepted. Refusing to return home, Francis hid in the priest's house, but his father found him and took him before the Bishop of Assisi to demand the return of his money. It was here that Francis made his dramatic gesture of renunciation of everything his father had represented to him. Standing naked before the Bishop, Francis mirrored the poor

Christ on trial. No power on earth could deflect him from the course he saw that God wanted him to take. There is no record that he was ever reconciled with his earthly father. Instead, claiming God as his only father,[7] Francis found the root of his being in God alone, finding his identity as brother to all the other creatures of God's world.

Come, Follow Me

With a characteristic flair for extremes, Francis thus came to embrace the life of the gospel with the same wholeheartedness he had previously dedicated to enjoying himself. Perhaps his preoccupation with literal poverty came partly from recognizing that his father's values and his own former lifestyle had not led anywhere real or satisfying. His freedom from possessions was also a freedom from distractions. Nothing, however good or desirable in its own right, could be allowed to divert him from God. Scholars may speculate on how the rich young man of the Gospel actually responded to Jesus' call to 'Go, sell all you have and give the money to the poor; then come, follow me.'[8] Francis' own response was never in doubt.

Francis was an all-or-nothing character in everything he did. He displayed the same singleness of mind and heart in his youthful pursuit of extravagance as in the frugality of his life after his conversion. In fact, an appetite for life in all its variety remains one of the central identifying marks of Franciscan living. Francis' insistence on a life of poverty and dependence may seem stark and uncompromising. His choice profoundly challenges the values of a materialistic world. Yet the way of Francis should never be allowed to become a sterile renunciation of that world or its people. Still less should it be a withdrawal from the life of the world out of hatred or fear of its reality. Even Franciscan hermits are deeply enmeshed in the concerns of the world through their prayer. Their lives, no less than lives of active service to the poor, are love in action. Franciscan spirituality is rooted in love for all things, and all people, as they *are*. The search for God in our lives begins with what already is, because everything in existence is already marked by the hand of God the Creator. There are plenty of signposts to the divine presence in our world, if only we have the perception to recognize them.

So how may Francis aid us in our search for a credible way forward in these times of global insecurity? There should be enough evidence already to show that Francis' relevance is not merely bound up with his own time or context. His attitude to the life of faith can teach us much about our own journeys and questions. Francis' love for God and all creation calls us *outward* from preoccupation with self, into connection and relationship with the world and its people. His devotion to the crucified Christ also calls us *inward*, to intimate communion with God our Creator, and to respond in passionate self-giving. His call to right relationship challenges us to think creatively about today's 'lepers': those we find it hardest to accept become, through this lens, our beloved brothers and sisters. We have already acknowledged something of the importance of learning to *listen* – to discern the presence of God at work in our world and in each other, to learn what he has in mind for us. Like Francis, we are called not just to follow Christ in outward observance, but to *become* Christlike. Further, we are to reflect back the image of Christ already alive in each person, by loving them and encouraging them into becoming the person they were uniquely called to be. The Good News is for all people, without exception. If we are prepared to listen, Francis can speak it with prophetic urgency for our time, as he did in his own.

Suggested Exercises

1. What is at the heart of your life? Is there anything about your priorities which you want, or need, to change? How might you go about this?

2. Are there any elements of Francis' own story which have particular resonance for you? What have been the memorable turning points or 'conversion moments' in your life?

3. Where are you completely committed (relationships, faith, work)? What holds you back from total commitment?

2

God with Us

Chiefest of all forms of service that the brothers and sisters can offer must ever be the effort to show others in his beauty and power the Christ who is the inspiration and joy of their own lives.

(*The Principles of the First Order of the Society of Saint Francis,* Day 22)

One of the chief hallmarks of the Franciscan way of life is its down-to-earth quality. The very phrase 'down-to-earth' sums up an essential element of Franciscan belief and practice. It is no longer possible to see God as remote, somewhere 'up there' out of the way. Since the birth of Jesus Christ, we have become aware that God's willingness to become incarnate connects him intimately with the life of every creature. God has walked this earth as one of us. This is the heart of the Christian mystery: God, limitless Creator of all things, submits to the limitation of human existence in order to demonstrate the truth of his love for us.

A Christ who is both truly God and truly human illumines our humanity by showing us what it is possible for a human to become. Saints are made when a human being accepts the challenge to grow beyond what we normally think of as the limits of human possibility.

Each of us is called to take seriously our status as creatures made in the image of the Creator. Each of us is called to reflect that image back to the world in which we live. Christians inherit the truth that in Jesus, God did not become flesh to live and die only once in a finite time and place, but for all time. Our flesh too contains the seeds of that mystery. We too can become more nearly like our Creator. We only have to want to. In striving to reflect God more perfectly, we become more perfectly human. Francis' life and spirituality are a potent example of this process at work.

Incarnational Presence

Since Francis' own time, two elements at the heart of the Franciscan life have been held in tension: the call to affirm the world by active, loving presence within it, and aloneness with God in contemplative withdrawal. Both elements are essential to any attempt to approach life as Francis did. When Francis withdrew to pray, he took with him the needs of those who might have no other access to God. And when Francis himself was praying alone for the world, his brothers and sisters, and those who came to be inspired by his message, were still in the midst of it, tackling with their presence the magnitude of human need. Both are important ways of living out the Franciscan vocation to be an incarnational presence in the world. For in both activities, prayer and work, Christians seek to do as Jesus did and to be, as nearly as they can, as he was.

All Christians are signs of God's presence, whether or

not it is recognized and interpreted as such by those among whom they live. Wherever someone of faith is, there is a reminder that people still seek to love and serve their God, and that God has not gone away. As in Francis' own time, though arguably for different reasons, the institutional Church today has in many places become remote from everyday human concerns. It can be perceived, rightly or wrongly, as having very little to do with the loving message of the gospel. People still need to know that they are loved, as they always have – but they no longer automatically trust the Church to be the bearer of that message. So people who live out their faith in an undramatic, down-to-earth way, communicating genuine love and humility, still have the capacity to reach hungry hearts, minds and souls with a sense of God's presence.

The leper who challenged Francis has never gone away. There are still people, existing rather than living on the margins of society, who desperately need someone to reach out to them in their isolation. Franciscans across the world continue to engage, together with others, in trying to communicate to them the reality of God's love. The materially secure 'post-Christian' citizens of the affluent West also need to hear that message of love. Modern life in the West has become so complex that there are signs of a renewed yearning for simplicity. There is growing recognition that a sense of purpose does not always accompany success. People want to be assured that their lives have meaning and worth. In the intense questioning that arose out of the events of 11 September, many who had never considered themselves religious came to ask whether there might be more lasting values than possession, accumulation and achievement. The 'little poor man' of Assisi, who called all people his brothers and sisters, is ideally placed to speak to our search for a solid base from which to live.

The Word Made Flesh

The birth of Christ is the most powerful reminder we have of God's reality. Every Christmas we are reminded that God loves us so much that he chooses to become known by us in a new way, by becoming one of us. The presence of God among us is made concrete, given a shape. Yet, despite God's terrifying power and majesty, the shape in which he chooses to become known as a human being reflects not might, but vulnerability. The defenceless child in the manger foreshadows that terrible human death at the hands of an occupying power. Yet this child, utterly dependent, is nevertheless truly God. H. R. Bramley's hymn sums it up beautifully:

> O wonder of wonders which none can unfold;
> The Ancient of Days is an hour or two old.[1]

Francis brought home this reality to the congregation of the church in Greccio, a village in the Rieti valley some way south of Assisi. One Christmas, he sought to re-create the scene of the stable in Bethlehem. Francis had brought into church all the props we associate with the Nativity: a cow, a donkey, hay, a manger, a real baby. To us, familiar with cribs of all varieties, this action has lost much of its impact. At least once a year these things become part of the paraphernalia of church or home; we are not surprised to see them, and may in fact have become so familiar with the sight that we stop really seeing it at all. To the people of Greccio, seeing it for the first time, it was a revelation. The everyday things of the world were invested with new holy meaning; these ordinary, everyday creatures were part of the story which God wants us all to hear and participate in. To them it was not a remote symbol to be grasped only through the powers of the intellect, but a visible, instantly comprehensible reminder that God is present with us everywhere, willing to be continually reborn for us and in us. Showing and preaching Christ's continued presence in the world in this very concrete way was central to Francis' ministry. His mission to rebuild the Church included making the faith real and accessible to its people.

The story of the crib at Greccio, as told by Francis' early biographers, highlights one more interesting fact about him: that he appears to have been ordained as a deacon and sometimes took the role, appropriate to the deacon, of reading the Gospel in the liturgy as he did at that particular Christmas service. We do not know when or by whom he was ordained; it is clear from the way he spoke and wrote about priests that he never aspired to become one himself. Instead, he again mirrors the calling of all Christians to follow in Jesus' footsteps. The Greek word *diakon* can be translated as 'servant'. The Jesus who took the role of a servant and washed his disciples' feet, despite their objections that this was unsuitable work for the Son of God, is the same Jesus who inspired

Francis to humble service of the outcasts of his time. The
Acts of the Apostles spells out in more detail the role of
deacons in the early Church, including making sure that
the poor of the parish were included and fed. Today, the
Church of England requires that deacons should be
ready to share in the Church's work of caring for the
poor, the needy and the sick. 'They are to strengthen the
faithful, search out the careless and the indifferent, and
to preach the word of God';[2] in short, to act as an incarnational presence in the world. Thus it is clear that
Francis did exercise a diaconal ministry, in the pattern of
the Servant Christ who humbled himself to share in our
humanity.[3]

Mind, Body and Spirit

In order to speak with any kind of integrity to people
who have no conception of what God is like, people of
faith need to live it honestly and openly. Our beliefs must
be consistent with everything we do, say or think; they
must influence every aspect of our lives and relationships. The tremendous reality of incarnation means that
there is no part of our human existence that cannot be
touched by God. There is no need for shame or evasion.
Jesus has been there before us. Every human emotion
and experience is infused with the presence of the divine.
Yet this approach, rooted in a sense of the goodness and
integrity of all creation, has not always been evident in
the teachings of the Church.

Today we are beginning at last to come to terms with
a different concept of bodiliness from that which would

have been understood in Francis' time. It is not always easy. Much Christian theology, from the time of the Desert Fathers onwards, had spoken of the body as inferior to the soul or spirit – it was messier, less easily controllable, constantly demanding. In much Christian thought, our bodies have been rejected as at best a distraction from the life of the Spirit, and at worst completely divorced from it. The spiritual realm was consistently portrayed as somehow higher than the physical; the spiritual body would be perfected only after death, and this life was merely a preparation for the life of the spirit. We are still living with the remnants of this attitude today. Yet it was into the physical form of a human infant that Christ was born. He did not reject the limitations of the human body. A fully incarnate Christ must necessarily have been physical, and sensual. From the Gospel accounts we know that he ate and drank, walked, rode donkeys. Touch was a vital part of his ministry of healing. He loved, wept, got angry. He died.

What does it really mean, then, that God created us physical beings? How do we live out to the full our call to become the Body of Christ today? A healthy Christian approach to our humanity should happily recognize our spiritual and physical reality as equally valid expressions of our Christlikeness. It could be argued that, despite the example of the incarnate Jesus, Christians believe what has been absorbed from Pauline theology about the opposition, rather than the integration, of body and spirit. Many of us are still uncomfortable with having bodies at all. This discomfort has become all too clear through the sorry mess we make of discussing anything

to do with gender or sexuality, for example. We attempt
to argue that Jesus was somehow exempt from that one
area of human embodiment; if he was a sexual being,
even in the broadest sense, we would really rather not
know about it. In fact, we secretly doubt that Jesus could
really have been flesh at all; if he truly was heir to the
same range of weaknesses and temptations that we are,
we would then have to be able to face up to them in ourselves rather than write them off as bad and not really of
God. In the same way, the fact that he was able to come
through human temptations without sinning forces us to
confront our own failures. So our vocation to be the
living Body of Christ is impaired, because we do not
want to envisage what that body might be like. It is all
too painful, and we find it easier to reduce the Body of
Christ to a picturesque symbol. However, the mystery of
the Incarnation calls us to contemplate the truth that
God became *flesh*, and that we are 'fearfully and wonderfully made'[4] in his image. Wholehearted membership
of the Body of Christ begins with the call to accept our
own physical embodiment, and rejoice that Jesus shared
it. It was our own human reality, however far from ideal,
that Jesus accepted and shared in his own body. Flesh
cannot be separated from mind or spirit if we are to see
ourselves as whole beings, and dedicate our whole selves
joyfully to God's service. Our human life and the
physical world in which we live can be the vessel for a
profound encounter with the love of God. In order to
become accurate reflections of the incarnate God, we
need to put *every* aspect of ourselves at God's disposal.
According to the *Principles* of the Anglican Society of

Saint Francis, for example, the balanced Franciscan life is made up of three 'ways of service':[5] prayer, study and work. Thus mind, body and spirit all find a place of equal value in the service of God.

The place of the mind in Franciscan life, however, has also given cause for dispute over the years. Although study quickly did become an accepted part of the ministry of the friars, and there were many learned Franciscan scholars, it is arguable that Francis himself was somewhat anti-intellectual. Certainly he was, at best, ambivalent about the benefits of academic learning. It played no part in the life he envisaged for the early brothers. The only book they needed to learn from was the Gospel. This attitude might in part be explained by the fact that literacy was then restricted to those who could afford it. Education was often available only through the very monasteries which had come to symbolize the Church's arrogance and detachment in their apparent rejection of the real world. To be 'unlettered', as Francis himself always claimed to be, was to be closer to the poor majority. Jesus and the disciples were simple people with little or no formal education. Francis knew that his Little Brothers would reflect that, coming as they did from a society in which the majority had no access to learning. From the start he was determined that they should *be* Little, or Lesser, Brothers. That acceptance of poverty and littleness affected every aspect of their life, both corporately and individually.

It is of course true that, even for academic theologians, writing, thinking or theorizing *about* God is no substitute for a direct personal relationship *with* him. Francis was right to distrust the glib games which can be played with truth, thus keeping it safe and manageable, unable to work its transformation. Having said all that, Francis himself displayed an unusual knowledge of Scripture. His writings also betray a familiarity with authors of the early Church, such as Jerome and Ambrose. In this too, of course, he resembles the Jesus who was able to argue with the learned men in the temple at a very early age. He also knew the Divine Office of the Church, presumably required of a deacon, and was able to marshal theological arguments of some complexity. His claim to be 'unlettered' is therefore somewhat disingenuous if taken literally. It was, however, entirely consistent with his desire to know God rather than know *about* him. The truth and reality of what is revealed about God in Scripture is paramount. God is real and knowable, not as arcane theory but as lived reality in relationship.

Francis' concern, with study as in all things, was that we need to rid ourselves of all the props that can shield us from living that reality ourselves. Poverty was about stripping off every cause for pride or self-absorption, everything that might draw the consciousness back from God to self. We are to become 'instruments of God's mighty working':[6] whatever we do is to be directed by God and to direct us back to him. In an article on Francis and poverty, an Anglican Franciscan brother tellingly remarks that as Francis saw it, a life of poverty 'must be a habitual reference to God, and such a life then really has no limits, because its dimensions are the dimensions of God'.[7]

All three of these ways of service, then, if held in

healthy balance, can become pointers to a Franciscan way of living in the world. Mind, body and spirit all need to be dedicated to the loving service of God. So, by persisting in prayer we learn to love the world and its people, by study we can aspire to understand it (which helps us in turn to love it more honestly), and by works we seek to do what we can to improve it, so that it mirrors more exactly the will of its Creator. Some brothers and sisters may find themselves drawn more to one aspect than another. There have been endless debates within the Franciscan movement, as in most other branches of Christianity, as to whether it is better to 'be' or to 'do'. The answer, is, naturally, both – but never to lose sight of God in attempting either.

Francis and 'Brother Ass'

Francis himself is not always the most obvious model for healthy ways to integrate body, mind and spirit. If there is one aspect of Francis which is hard to grasp today, it is his apparent thirst for self-mortification and self-denial. This typically medieval approach, so admired by his early biographers as a sure sign of his holiness, can seem exaggerated, or even neurotic, to the contemporary mind. 'Denying yourself' seems to go against the grain of all current wisdom. We have got used to assuming that our rights should be respected and our needs met. It is, fortunately, commonplace now for Christians to employ the insights of psychology, along with theology, in the quest for maturity as complete persons made in God's image. We are thus aware that in order to grow and flourish as full human beings, we must recognize our needs and desires, for it can ultimately prove damaging not to do so. In what way, then, can it make sense to embrace a Franciscan path of self-denial?

In the light of modern thought, Francis' approach to 'Brother Ass', as he slightingly referred to his body, can seem irresponsible, a waste of one of God's more obvious gifts. He often denied it adequate food and clothing. He was zealous to the point of obsession about renouncing every detail of the soft, luxurious life in which he had been brought up. Yet it was not out of hatred of the body that Francis adopted this attitude. Instead, his approach is all of a piece with his love of poverty. It is especially important to grasp that to Francis, 'body' was a broader concept than simply the physical frame in which his spirit lived. It encompassed 'everything we want for ourselves, and undertake because of love of self rather than love of God and our fellow human beings'.[8] In that context it becomes easier to understand (if not to imitate) Francis' refusal to give in to any desire or need his body might communicate.

Nakedness and apparent humiliation crop up frequently in stories of Francis. From the moment in the bishop's court when he stripped off every piece of clothing his father had given him, nakedness for Francis became a sign of extreme vulnerability. Defenceless, with nowhere to hide, he was forced to confront directly the truth of his dependence on God alone. Any hint of pride or presumption in ourselves could be swiftly put in its place by a reminder that we have nothing in this world we can legitimately call our own. Francis was concerned to be utterly consistent in his pursuit of poverty of self. It is God from whom we receive all we have; everything, including life itself, is gift. We can fantasize as much as we like about being able to buy control over our lives. It is not possible, however, to purchase immunity from God. So Franciscan poverty has to be lived out in every fibre of our being. In every relationship with the things we use to feed and clothe ourselves, the people who meet our need for companionship and intimacy, we are to see the deeper truth of our dependence on God.

Our own understanding of poverty may be deepened, in this materially obsessed age, if we are prepared to consider honestly the way we use words like 'want' and 'need'. The way of Francis permits no self-deception. The driving force of Franciscan poverty is an emptying of self in order to be open to God. Acknowledging our true needs is one thing; being possessed and controlled by them is quite another. Practising self-denial is of little value if it does not encourage us to look beyond self; if we feel diminished by what we do not have, we are not yet free to embrace the poverty of Christ in the way that Francis did.

So much of our identity is bound up with possession; we define who we are, at least in part, by the things we have, or the people over whom we exercise control. We want more control, so we desire more things. In order to justify acquiring the newest, the fastest, the smartest, we tell ourselves that we *need* them. For centuries before Francis' birth into the emerging mercantile class, status had been conferred by ownership of precious and beautiful objects. As trade grew in importance, emphasis was

beginning to shift away from the objects themselves
to the money they generated. Merchants like Pietro
Bernardone could buy political power which had not, up
till that time, been guaranteed them by birthright. The
accident of birth was an indicator of good fortune, and
even of divine favour; God was assumed to be in favour
of the status quo. Little could be done about the family
into which you were born, but in acquiring money and
possessions, you could buy significance in the eyes of the
world, and believe that God had blessed your endeavours. Little has changed: money is power, we are told,
and if it can't buy you love or happiness, it can purchase
enough compensations to keep you from noticing the
emptiness inside.

Francis' life represents a radical challenge to this set of
values. His rejection of his father's name, of wealth and
power, set him free to find his own definitions. He
was no longer to be valued for what he owned, but for
who he was. His refusal to be limited or defined by
objects highlights the desperation with which we seek
to understand ourselves by rushing to accumulate more
things. Francis was content simply to be himself, entirely
unencumbered by the pressure of ownership or control
over anything, including his own physical self. By relinquishing control to God, he was set free to live in right
relationship with all things. This freedom and simplic
ity still attracts many. As patron saint of ecology, in
particular, Francis' way of co-existing with his fellow
creatures can be a potent reminder of our urgent need to
renegotiate our own relationship with creation. We
cannot continue to exploit and abuse other creatures as

we did when we assumed resources were infinite. As we celebrate the privilege of our incarnation in God's image, we are beginning to recognize the responsibility that comes with it. God did not abandon his creation after it was made. Instead, he is continually present, still making and remaking. We are called to share in the work of creation by concern for the other creatures. Francis' non-possessive response to that gift is a vital model for an age of greed and global warming.

'Francis, rebuild my church'

When Francis wrote a Rule for his brothers in the early years of the thirteenth century, it differed in important ways from the monastic rules which existed before that time. We will look at the Rules in more detail in later chapters. Perhaps the most striking difference is in the size; the sixth-century Rule of St Benedict runs to seventy-three chapters, while Francis' Rule of 1223 comprises just twelve. Francis' interpretation of what it meant to live the life of the gospel was pared down to essentials. There were fewer structures than in a conventional monastic community, hence less need to be prescriptive about how the brothers were to relate to them. The keystone of Francis' own life, and by extension that of his brothers, was the attempt to follow Christ as literally as he could. This literalism is clearly visible in his response to his experience of hearing Jesus' voice from the crucifix at San Damiano. In his eagerness to respond to Jesus' call to 'rebuild my church', Francis missed the nuance of what he was really being asked to do. He did rebuild the church, physically, with stones paid for with his father's cloth. Only then did he come to understand the symbolic aspect of this same call – there was also a need to rebuild the Church with love, with active service and with preaching. Even as he grasped and responded to this new awareness, Francis continued in his literal response of making physical improvements to churches. It was indeed important to give people a place to worship, and to build up their sense of worth by repairing the building at the heart of their community. Yet it is arguably in the second, more symbolic sense that Francis really made a lasting contribution to the renewal of the Church.

As we have seen, it was in a world oddly similar to our own that Francis' gospel living had its initial impact. Money was in the ascendant everywhere. The Church had become too rich and too powerful to connect effectively with people's everyday lives. It had allowed itself to become caught up with the trappings of secular power and status, and had lost its integrity as it became increasingly divorced from the itinerant carpenter and fishermen who had brought it to birth. Through Francis and those who followed in his pattern of gospel living, the Church rediscovered its foundations. Many times since, it has appeared to be in danger of forgetting them again. But while the Church may need to adjust to new ways of engaging with a world characterized by rapid change, people still hear and respond to the call to rebuild its essence according to the pattern of Christ.

The literal and the symbolic intertwined powerfully again towards the end of Francis' life, as he sought to enter into the passion of Christ through his prayer on the mountain of La Verna. He could not actually ask to be crucified; after all, even St Peter had refused to be crucified the same way up as his Lord. However, he could ask to know for himself what Christ suffered. In the granting of this request, Francis received the gift of the stigmata, the marks of the nails in his hands, feet and side. Thus he journeyed as far as is possible for any mortal along the path Christ took. His own physical suffering was, to an extent, chosen or accepted, as Christ's had been. It would not be the way for everyone; not even Francis' own brothers were always able to understand the extremes of his response to Christ's passion. For the literal-minded Francis, however, it was clear that this was the way he had to go. In his meditations on the passion, Francis was truly taking up his own cross in order to follow as far as he could.

Extreme experiences such as the stigmata may seem to push Francis beyond our reach. We cannot aspire to such a perfect identification with the person and passion of Christ. However, Francis, though saintly, was also only human – and very aware of his frailty. Because a human being has done it already, we have proof that it *would* be possible to follow Christ to the utmost limits. We could do it ourselves; we would only have to want to do so, more than we wanted anything else. In order to go where Francis went, we have to put all concept of self-fulfilment aside. Desire, for Francis, was focused solely on God. Understanding God's will was not a dry intellectual exercise, but a striving of mind, heart, body and soul to become indissoluble from God.

Christ himself prayed in the Garden of Gethsemane for God's will, not his own human one, to be done. We are used to saying to God 'your will be done', but we usually fail to pray it as though we mean it. Without at least a dash of Francis' literalism, it is easy to escape its real impact. The poverty and vulnerability implicit in surrendering our will to God are too costly. Instead of a real openness to God's will, we tend to prefer to hang on to the illusion that it is we who are in control. The ultimate cost of praying 'your will be done' is usually more than we are willing to pay. But the message of the cross is universal. The crucifix at San Damiano which spoke so powerfully to Francis does not just show the figure of Christ alone on the cross. Grouped around him are his mother, disciples, angels and other figures. In this way we come to recognize that Christ's passion, like his birth, includes us all. He opens our human flesh to new possibilities by being born as one of us; by dying and rising, he removes more barriers between ourselves and God. Even if being open to God's will does involve us in suffering and death like his, we will not be alone. The Kingdom is no longer a distant prospect, but a reality rooted as firmly in our own world as it is in heaven.

The Suffering Body of Christ

Even as we come to embrace more honestly the way of self-denial, it is important to stress that pain is not of itself good. Instead of ennobling and stretching our humanity towards God in imitation of the crucified Christ, it can often shrink us to a smaller, meaner, more self-centred version of what we once were. Yet Francis, along with countless contemplatives down the ages, showed that it is somehow possible to absorb and transform some of the world's pain in the passion of Christ. In seeking to enter as closely as he could into Christ's own suffering, he was able to hold that pain and need before God. He trusted that, again like Christ, his gift of himself might be turned to good use in the service of God's suffering people.

Our own response to the endless reporting of human need on the news is often to feel helpless. There seems so little we can do. We do not know how, or whether, to pray. We cannot frame the right words. All we are left with is a cry for help, perhaps for understanding. *Make it come right, please, God,* we cry out as the disciples must have cried on Good Friday when it seemed nothing would ever come right again. Yet we are also called to journey into the heart of that wrongness, for there we find God, waiting to burst forth into new life.

So we return to the events of 11 September. A great evil, born of more great evil, till it is impossible to untangle the mess of guilt and responsibility. The complexity of ancient hatreds, allowed to feed for centuries on real and imagined wrongs. A saddened and chastened world, shocked for once into contemplating new ways of living and caring for our environment and those who share it with us. A God trying to reach out to us through his own experience of pain, vulnerability and loss. And an urgent call not to lash out at the nearest likely target, but to listen, to pray, to engage in the costly struggle for understanding and justice. In the events of that day we confronted the previously unimaginable. Those who saw themselves as powerless used terrible power to strike at the heart of the American identity: its tall towers, its wealth, its military might. With whom do we identify in such events? If this was what it took to awaken our compassion and our thirst for justice, what does that say about our attitude to all those who have died in previous atrocities? Has an obsession with understanding this one event underlined our humanity, or our failure to recognize the humanity of all those whose death came in other conflicts which did not touch so painfully our own sense of identity?

Everybody is diminished by terrorism, wherever it occurs and whoever is the perpetrator. There the previously powerless find their voice by striking back at their oppressors, by choosing to oppress and destroy in turn. Nobody is really empowered by violence, however satisfying at the moment it happens, however compelling the drive for revenge. Instead a cycle of hate is created. Voices of reason and of love are not heard above the sound of military hardware and political rhetoric. Even God has no power, no voice, in such a situation but what we allow him. The still small voice of calm is a compelling image when we have the space and the luxury to listen. But in order to respond with a Franciscan Christlikeness to that still small voice, we need to *want* to hear it when other sounds are louder.

Francis sought to respond to powerlessness and poverty in others, and to crave it for himself. But terror was not his way. He spent his life with the powerless, but he worked to rebuild and affirm, not to destroy and humiliate. Leprosy is not cured by making the lepers live a long way away, or denying them their humanity. Instead, their potentially destructive isolation is tackled with an embrace, by being present rather than running away. Francis' way is truly the way of Christ – of incarnational presence, being content to *be* with the suffering, needy and voiceless of our world as Christ was content to be one of us. His way is the way of loving transformation, of listening, of allowing possibilities to become reality. With Francis, we become aware that we are called to be more than we are. We are called to transcend the human differences and difficulties which hold us back from full communion and understanding of one another.

> Francis, in the poor and foolish
> Of the world community
> Celebrating all creation,
> Show us how we all might be.
>
> Through the wounds that you were granted
> Sharing with the world's despised,
> Outcast, help us live your vision,
> Always by God's love surprised.
>
> Help us meet the wolf within us,
> Fears we cannot bear to name;
> Grant us strength to overcome them,
> Courage not to stay the same.
>
> Help us live that urgent calling,
> Trusting God will make us free,
> In commitment to each other
> Being, in simplicity.

Francis, help us to go deeper,
See, beyond the birds and flowers,
Through your joy in God's creation
Greater truths that must be ours.[9]

Suggested Exercises

1. Make your own crib scene, using any objects you like. How do you choose to represent the world in which you meet the God made flesh?

2. Practise becoming aware of your body in preparation for prayer. Adopt a comfortable posture which you can hold without strain. Breathe slowly and regularly in and out. Be aware of the points of contact between your body and the floor or furniture.

3. You might like to take regular inventories of the things around you. If you haven't worn, read or used it for a year, do you really need it?

3

Gospel Living

Most high, glorious God, enlighten the darkness of my heart
And give me true faith, certain hope and perfect charity,
sense and knowledge, Lord,
that I may carry out your holy and true command.

(St Francis' Prayer before the Crucifix)[1]

Francis is famously alleged to have told his brothers to go out and preach the gospel, adding, 'if necessary, use words'. Words, he was saying, need to be harnessed to action if they are to have meaning. They need to be given life through the living presence of the Word made flesh. Gospel living needs to communicate and share the Good News by which we live. We must be consistent in living, as Francis did, according to the good news that God, in Jesus, has come to be with us and will never leave us.

Following the Gospel

Francis didn't set out to found an order. Although some of the early brothers, at least, were his friends, Francis did not want followers for himself, drawn by his own personality. Instead, they came because they saw in him something of the love of Christ who motivated and compelled him. Those who were tempted to remark on his special qualities found themselves exhorted to look beyond him to Christ. For Francis' original intention was simply to follow Christ as literally as he could in response to hearing the gospel. As Francis sought to live his own life of poverty and chastity in obedience to God, an order grew up around him, almost by default: as he says in his *Testament*, 'When God gave me brothers, there was nobody to tell me what I should do'.[2] As the little group of brothers grew, so they began to require some way to regulate their existence. When their numbers reached eleven, somewhere around 1210, Francis wrote the first of his Rules for the Friars Minor, or Little Brothers. His Rule of 1223 begins with the assertion that the Rule and Life of the friars is 'to observe the Holy Gospel of Our Lord Jesus Christ'.[3] The mechanics of the emergent order were secondary to its firm purpose of re-creating the life of the gospel in their own time.

Echoing Jesus' disciples, the brothers asked Francis to teach them to pray, for many of them were unfamiliar with the office (prayer book) of the Church, which had long been the preserve of priests and monks. In response, Francis taught them to say the Our Father and the Prayer on Entering a Church, still used in Franciscan churches and chapels around the world:

We adore you, most holy Lord Jesus Christ,
here and in all your churches throughout the whole
   world;

and we bless you, because by your holy cross
you have redeemed the world.[4]

Francis' rule names the three vows of poverty, chastity
and obedience as the *way* in which the friars are to live
the life of the gospel. These three vows are also known as
the 'evangelical counsels', reflecting their gospel basis.
Mirroring aspects of the life of Christ who lived without
possessing or exploiting, they are designed to set free,
rather than to restrain or constrict. They are not about
'don'ts', focused on the negative. Much more important
is what they have to say about power. The Franciscan
way is about the healthy renunciation of power; not an
immature escape from responsibility, but the refusal to
seek protection from the consequences of the call to follow Christ. Poverty, chastity and obedience are a choice
for all Christians not to exercise power over things. Even
our own bodies, the direction of our lives or the lives of
others – all that we have and all that we are is to be put
at *God's* disposal, not at our own. In thus accepting
the full weight of Jesus' prayer to his Father, 'Your will,
not mine, be done', we open ourselves to a paradox.
As Archbishop Rowan Williams said to a gathering of
Anglican religious communities: 'The inseparability of
utter cost and utter joy is something that should worry
people about Christianity, it's so blindingly unobvious.'[5]
Freedom and joy are found in powerlessness, in identifying with those who have no choice about their own lack
of power. In the values of the gospel, abundant life
comes not through circumventing pain and defenceless-
ness, but in embracing it as Jesus did.

Gospel Living as Radical Response

There is a desperate need today for the Church to rediscover its own credibility. Christians are uncertain how to
live in the real world without betraying or compromising
the countercultural values of the faith. It is probably fair
to say that in the West, generally speaking, Christians
are currently failing to get across the message that we are
still human beings despite the fact that we live according
to a religion. We have not been able to communicate the
idea that to live according to gospel values is to live as a
complete human, rather than to have bits cut out of our
personality in order to fit a stereotype. People find it
impossible to believe that our creed can offer any joy for
our lives, or any hope for theirs. Far from being 'worried' or challenged by Christianity, many have simply
rejected it because our inability to live it as it should be
lived shows them so little of its potential.

There are vast numbers who believe in God without
finding any need for an institutional church to broker
their relationship with God; this fact should alert those
of us inside the institution that the Word we live by has
somehow become dissociated from the *way* we live. It
seems we are not sharing the good news of God very
effectively. Yet a church which has total confidence in
itself can risk tipping over into arrogance, the domineer-
ing assumption of control over people's lives. Power and
control can easily become confused; it is God in whom
we should have confidence, not in our own structures.
We have lost the power and status we once had as the
Church, and with it a lot of our confidence; but that gives

us a great opportunity to speak with real significance to many who feel the same way about their own lives.

Does it matter if we look ridiculous to the world in the attempt to live by our topsy-turvy values? We may feel we need to act in a certain way in order to be credible in the eyes of the world. There is much scope for disagreement about what that certain way might be. Francis' way was to act with integrity in wholehearted pursuit of the truth of God, and to let that speak for him. It is risky to take on the powers of the world. To attempt to model a different way leaves us open to charges of hypocrisy and much else. Standing up for our values, when we are faced with so much that ridicules and dismisses them, makes us acutely aware of our littleness and our vulnerability. But Francis' life has opened up the possibility that the same littleness and vulnerability are precisely where we encounter God most fully; when our defences are down and we are aware of our dependence, then God has a chance to do something with us.

Francis' response to hearing the Word of God in the reading of the Gospel was immediate, yet very deep-rooted. The compulsion he felt at the call to 'sell all you have, give to the poor and come, follow me'[6] was strong enough to silence the part of him which had previously enjoyed luxury, as well as the rational part which must have known his decision would cause trouble with his father. Even before Francis was aware himself of the depth of his vocation to emulate Christ, parallels between them were emerging. For example, Francis' confrontation with his father before the bishop echoed Jesus' response as the adolescent runaway found by his anxious parents in the temple at Jerusalem. As Jesus says to Mary, 'Did you not know I must be in my Father's house?',[7] we hear Francis declaring to the court that he has no earthly father. The imperative of the gospel was strong enough to override any sense of family loyalty or obligation; to be limited to being a Bernardone would have been a betrayal of Francis' deeper sense that his true identity was to be found only in God.

This paradox illustrates why gospel values are so hard to take on wholeheartedly. They turn our ideas upside down, contradict our perceptions of what is important, and draw out of us resources that it would be more comfortable to keep hidden even from ourselves. The foolishness of God, we are told, is wiser than any human wisdom.[8] In the Magnificat, Mary's great song when she is first acknowledged as the mother of the Lord, those upside-down values are given voice. The promise of the Kingdom is no longer only a distant hope. In the child in Mary's womb, in his life among us and our own attempts to follow in his way, it is becoming a reality now.

A Person Without a Teapot

Franciscan spirituality, as we have seen, has been lived out from the beginning in incarnational presence among those in need. However, it can be difficult to find appropriate ways of being there. 'Just being' sounds easy, but if it is done in the true spirit of the gospel, it is intensely costly. People on the margins, like Francis' lepers, are still people. They do not need patronizing with the assumption that you are here to help, or that *you* are the person who has something to offer. More, they do not need any assumption as to who is 'normal', or healthy, or holy; of who really belongs out on the edges of the acceptable, and who might just be visiting. Words, here, mean little. Words distance us from the experience of having nothing to say. And words will fail to make much impression unless they are backed up with some form of consistent living. Even the Word itself, if forced on people aggressively or in lieu of practical help, will probably be able to achieve relatively little.

The story of Job's comforters has become a byword for striking uselessness in pastoral care. Their theological constructs do not touch Job's experience. When they start to speak, their advice misses the point; they come nowhere near to assuaging Job's suffering. However, before they ruin everything with their well-intentioned words, their initial reaction is very different. When they first hear of the terrible things Job has endured, they decide to go to him; and when they arrive they sit down on the ground beside him in silence for a week, 'for they saw that his suffering was very great'.[9] This silent companionship is incarnational presence at work.

An Anglican Franciscan sister from London tellingly describes[10] how she found herself faced with this dilemma when she first became involved with homeless people trying to overcome dependence on alcohol. She observed that there was an unspoken competition going on among the volunteers to be the one who took round the teapot or the soup ladle; if you had a visible job to do, you did not have to engage with the homeless people except as a provider. Meeting them without props or a defined role was much more demanding. Without a teapot, you were just another person; no better, no worse, than those among whom you sat. There was nothing to protect you from the torrent of pain which was most people's story; nothing to shield you from accusations of do-gooding or voyeurism, 'slumming it' among the less fortunate in order to feel virtuous at no personal cost.

Making soup or pouring tea also has visible results. It is easier to pretend to yourself that you have done *some-thing*, however small, than when all you have been able to do is to sit alongside someone in pain, with nothing to offer but the act of being there and not walking away. In places of such acute need, a teapot or soup ladle becomes a safety net with which people's pain can be kept at arm's length in order to make it bearable. To have a role, even a small and apparently menial one, makes it possible to believe that there is a difference between the 'carer' and the 'cared-for'. It can become an excuse not to enter into or identify with the *experience* of the 'cared-for'. When the teapot is taken away, there is nothing left but direct encounter with people. Most of us would be afraid to make ourselves that vulnerable. For each of us is afraid of rejection, no matter who is dealing it out. Many people who have worked in caring professions would admit a complicated set of motivations and responses to the people among whom they work. Compassion and the desire for justice combine with darker, less easily admissible feelings of helplessness and anger, frustration, and even envy. A life with nothing can appear paradoxically seductive: those in need have, without necessarily wanting anything of the sort, achieved a simplicity which the more secure may secretly yearn for.

I recognize very well the temptation to avoid the discomfort of life-without-a-teapot. For the first twenty-something years of my life I was an academic high flyer. In much of the work I have done since, this fact has been an irrelevance, if not an actual hindrance. Being alongside people, meeting them face on without theorizing, without distancing myself consciously or unconsciously behind a wall of words, is very hard for me. Yet it is that sense of recognition that lay at the heart of my own exploration of the Franciscan way of living the gospel in community, a way I took for just over seven years.

Before joining the Franciscans, I lived and worked for a number of years with people who have severe physical and mental disabilities. Like homeless people, they often provoke the response: 'I couldn't do that'; fear, often the fear of being asked to acknowledge that we too are broken and disabled in a variety of less obvious ways, gets in the way of encounter. Yet here too, there is a deep truth which has enriched many of us who have dared to become vulnerable enough to enter their world, even for a short time. As Rose's article puts it, we need places for the 'non-survivors' of the world we have created around achievement and acquisition; 'places where the fragile, broken and vulnerable can live to their full potential, places where to succeed means simply to be yourself'.[11]

The L'Arche communities for people with learning

disabilities strive to be one such oasis for broken people. Founded in France in the 1960s, these communities are now worldwide. In some countries people with disabilities are still looked on as a curse from God, in response to some sin or failure on the part of their parents; rejected by their families, some live in cages or on the streets. Even in supposedly more enlightened countries, people who are 'different' encounter a great deal of prejudice and rejection. Many have spent years in institutions. In the L'Arche communities they are welcomed, recognized as individuals, their gifts celebrated and their personhood nurtured. In this atmosphere, L'Arche (French for ark) offers a home, welcome and acceptance for as long as it is needed, both to those with an obvious disability and to the ostensibly 'normal', who may come at first wishing to help and end up by recognizing how very much they have to learn. Real relationship and intimacy are built up between people whose backgrounds and life experiences have nothing in common.

The ark is both a place of safety, a place where people are enabled to sail away from previous experience of abuse and rejection, and a place of challenge; nobody believed that there could be any sense in Noah building his boat until the rains began. The ark, too, contains something precious, like the Ark of the Covenant; and like both those first arks, it is on a journey of hope across hostile terrain. There is a great deal in common between the spirituality of L'Arche and the spirituality of Franciscans; indeed, the L'Arche community in Liverpool was the birthplace of my own Franciscan vocation. The two share a vocabulary of poverty and littleness, and an understanding of the basic truth of our shared humanity. In the theology of L'Arche, as in the Franciscan life, every other human being is my brother or sister, and I cannot say that their pain and need are not my concern. But the tone of everyday life, while not overlooking need and suffering, is nevertheless celebratory. The promise of the Magnificat is still with us; in its recitation each evening, we can receive a daily reminder that the poor *will* be lifted high and the hungry fed. Indeed, where people are learning to succeed by being themselves, it is happening already.

Living the gospel calls us into *engagement* with our world and its people, at any level from the meeting of individuals in need to the reform of whole systems. How do we go about transforming the ideal into the real? The above description of two different kinds of ministry, and their interplay with Franciscan vocation, may sound hopelessly idealized. The day-to-day reality of life in any kind of community, however, is often very far from ideal. Life in a community dedicated to welcoming the broken is perhaps even more costly, because it is so obvious when you fail. There is no escape from the expensive vulnerability of being alongside people who know exactly how broken you are yourself, and exactly where your wounds are most sensitive. It is not clear from moment to moment who has the teapot: when those considered poor by conventional standards are lifted high, and the mighty humbled, it is not always easy to work out where you fit in. Community on Franciscan lines should always be alive in this way with the upside-down values of the gospel. Because the community, by definition, is made up of broken human beings, the ideal is often glimpsed only faintly in the distance.

Make Me a Channel of Your Peace

During my time as a Franciscan, it was not uncommon to undertake some engagement on the community's behalf, only to be confronted with somebody singing 'Make me a channel of your peace'. In actual fact, the song is nothing at all to do with Francis. The words are from a prayer which originated in France in the nineteenth century; it seems to have become linked with Francis when a prayer card was produced for soldiers in the trenches of World War I, with the words of the prayer on one side and a picture of St Francis on the other. It is very much the sort of thing which Francis *might* have written, so it is not perhaps surprising that it should have become so firmly connected with him. Certainly, it echoes the language of his *Admonitions*, a series of meditative passages on scriptural themes:

> Where there is charity and wisdom,
>   there is neither fear nor ignorance.
>
> Where there is patience and humility,
>   there is neither anger nor disturbance.
>
> Where there is poverty with joy,
>   there is neither greed nor avarice.
>
> Where there is rest and meditation,
>   there is neither anxiety nor restlessness.

Where there is fear of the Lord to guard an entrance
there the enemy cannot have a place to enter.

Where there is a heart full of mercy and discernment,
there is neither excess nor hardness of heart.[12]

Even if the phrase itself is not Francis' own, however, his
vocation to *become* a channel of peace is important to
our understanding of his contemporary relevance. The
Beatitudes challenge us to become peacemakers in the
pattern of Christ; but we also know what is demanded of
those who become true children of God.

Peacemaking was a major part of Francis' way of
living out his commitment to the gospel. The 'taming'
of the wolf of Gubbio is often presented as another
picturesque example of Francis' ability to connect with
animals. In actual fact, though its central character is a
wolf, it is not really an animal story. Instead, and much
more vitally, it is a powerful example of Francis' call to
reconciliation and dialogue. The town of Gubbio, some
way north of Assisi, was being terrorized by a hungry
wolf. It ate the sheep that grazed outside the town, and
the people were afraid to go out in case they were next;
they had tried to hunt and kill the wolf, but with no
success. Hearing this, Francis took pity on them, and
decided to go out and meet the wolf himself. The townspeople tried to dissuade him, fearing that the wolf would
attack and kill him too. But Francis went out to the
wolf's lair. He made it clear to the wolf that it would be
wrong to eat people 'for they are made in the image of
God', but nevertheless offered a peace deal, based on the

transformation of attitudes on both sides. Recognizing that the wolf's actions had sprung from its hunger, Francis promised to persuade the people to put out food for it and stop hunting it with their dogs if the wolf would agree not to threaten the people or eat their sheep. The wolf agreed that it would abide by the deal, and they returned together to the town. As Francis publicly asked the wolf to make good its promise never again to hurt another creature, the wolf showed its acceptance of the pledge by placing its paw in Francis' hand. In return, it is said that the people of Gubbio kept their side of the bargain and fed the wolf, and that he became a kind of mascot for them, keeping intruders away from the town.

Strikingly, Francis found ways to communicate with the wolf across barriers of language and species. Though he did not condone its murderous activities, he sought to reassure the wolf that he did understand the need that lay behind the unacceptable behaviour, and so established dialogue. The wolf was not 'tamed'; it never became less than a wolf. Francis' solution was to recognize the need that drove it, and to find ways of meeting that need which did not involve exploitation or the abuse of power. And throughout the account, Francis called the wolf 'Brother', thus underlining a sense of relatedness rather than of separation or superiority. In these simple ways, Francis therefore modelled some of the essential aspects of peace and reconciliation work in any age. If peace is to be built on solid foundations, some common ground must first be established; any wish for revenge must be overcome by a willingness to co-operate, so that the past does not strangle the future.

Whatever the literal truth of the story of Francis and the wolf, it illustrates something of Francis' ability to enter a potentially explosive situation with only his faith and simplicity as a resource. Apparently somewhat naively, he goes to reconcile two sides driven apart by mutual fear and resentment. Human history shows that such attempts are not usually successful; however much we might want to believe in a way forward, cynicism often seems to shout louder than simplicity. However, even in the most complex and painful situations of our recent history, seeds of hope are to be found in similar small, risky gestures. Integrated schools and camps in Ireland and parts of the Middle East encourage at least some to begin the same process of recognition; if we get to know other people, we are less likely to be over-powered by our need to fear them and be rid of them.

Loving your enemies, as Jesus demands that we learn to do, requires that we see them as other human beings, rather than aliens or monsters qualitatively different from ourselves. Learning to understand why they do the things that hurt and diminish us is far more costly than retaliating – yet if we are ever to accept our enemy as brother or sister, we have to enter their world and be prepared to be vulnerable in welcoming them into ours. As with the lepers Francis came to see as images of Christ, or the homeless and disabled people whose pain still challenges our faith in a loving God, the barriers have to come down. Only by renouncing power, daring to become defenceless, by risking all in order to make connections, can we truly live the gospel of love and reconciliation.

Francis and Islam

Another striking thing about Francis, by comparison
with other Christians of his period, was his willingness
to enter into *dialogue* with Muslims, when the rest of
the Christian West was trying to kill them. The parallel
with today is obvious. Some parts of society, even
within Christian circles, are in danger of forgetting
the prophetic witness of Francis and others down the
ages who have chosen dialogue when others were
wedded to violence. One small good which has come
out of the appalling deaths of so many on 11 September
and its aftermath is that many have been led to
study the Qu'ran for the first time, trying to understand
the culture and mindset of those it might be easier to
hate.

Perhaps there is another story of conversion here. Like
others of his time, Francis seems initially to have set off
to meet the Sultan in the belief that his way was superior.
And there was never any question of surrender to the
details of the Muslims' religious belief. Francis remained
always convinced that Christ is the Way, but instead of
attempting to force that on those with whom he spoke,
he listened and learned from the integrity with which
they lived out their own faith. In fact, the language of
surrender and victory is inappropriate here: what was
going on was *exchange*. Francis was welcomed and
encouraged by the Sultan's hospitality, an approach he
would have recognized from his own way of dealing
with strangers, and so came to respect, if not share, his
beliefs and values. He did not try to destroy the oppos-

ition, but to live out his belief in a common humanity. If the Sultan and his people would not have been comfortable with the concept of being made in the image of God (for Allah is so holy that any attempt to depict him is blasphemy), they would at least have recognized Francis' insistence on our connection to each other through our common relationship to one God.

After 11 September, politicians commonly took refuge in rhetoric which threatened any prospect of lasting peace between the West and the Islamic world. In the midst of this climate, Pope John Paul II invited leaders of all the world's major religions to gather in Assisi for a day of prayer for world peace. One of the Muslim representatives, Kamel al-Sharif of the International Islamic Council for Da'wa and Relief, spoke of St Francis as 'a symbol of universal dialogue, because he highlighted the fact that truth is never only on one side'. Such a response to a person whose views are not only different but potentially dangerous may seem challenging, painful, even threatening to our current culture. We like to think of ourselves as tolerant and multicultural. Under that veneer, however, lurks a less edifying truth. We are used to despising and rejecting those who are alien to our cherished values; once again, as Christians in a secular world, we find ourselves caught between the dictates of our religion ('Love your enemies') and the demands of pragmatism ('they will destroy us unless we find a way to control them'). The way of reconciliation is not always popular in such a climate, because of the cost involved. If we admit our enemies are human beings as we are, we will have to acknowledge their needs, fears and rights as equivalent to our own. Such simplicity is not easily achieved.

Humility, we are told in the quotation at the very beginning of this Part, is 'a recognition of the truth about God and ourselves'. Accommodating other points of view into our own way of dealing with the world requires a lot of honesty and self-awareness; listening with an open mind and heart to the story of another individual, another faith or culture, demands humility. There is nothing more dangerous than the arrogance of refusing to believe we have anything to learn. Francis showed us a possible way to make that humility achievable for us. He remained committed to dialogue – to keeping communication going and not allowing estrangement to creep in. We are not to remain or become strangers to each other, but are to recognize and celebrate our interconnectedness as brothers and sisters, children of the same heavenly Father. And with recognition comes the responsibility to value each other and the world we share. In our modern world, we need more than ever to recognize where and to whom we belong.

So what, ultimately, is the good news we proclaim? In the words of Meister Eckhart: 'The seed of God is in us. Now, the seed of a pear tree grows into a pear tree; and a hazel seed grows into a hazel tree; a seed of God grows into God.'[13] God is already at work in us and through us. Gospel values are costly and demanding; but adhering to them in all our relating will bring us closer to Francis' vision of wholeness for ourselves, our Church and our world.

Suggested Exercises

1. What is the essence of the Good News for you? Can Francis offer any insights which might help you communicate this good news in the way you live your life?

2. Are there any individuals or groups of people from whom you instinctively recoil, as Francis did from lepers? Why do you react to them in such a way? Think of some *practical* ways which might help you enter into their experience of the world and see in them something of Christ's reality.

Part Two
Love

The Master says, 'By this everyone will know that you are my disciples, if you have love for one another'.[1] Love is thus the distinguishing feature of all true disciples of Christ. It must be specially an outstanding note in the lives of those who are seeking to be specially consecrated to Christ as his servants. God is love and, for those whose lives are hidden with Christ in God, love will be the very atmosphere which surrounds all that they do.

(*The Principles of the First Order of the Society of Saint Francis*, Day 27)

4

Poverty

The Master willingly embraced a life of poverty. He was rich, yet for your sake he became poor. He chose a stable for his birthplace and for his upbringing the house of a village carpenter. Even that home he left in early manhood and became a wayfarer, with nowhere to lay his head. Us also he calls to poverty. . . . 'None of you can become my disciple if you do not give up all your possessions'.

(*The Principles of the First Order of the Society of Saint Francis*, Day 5)

We live in a world dizzied by choice. We have grown used to the idea that we can have what we want, and indeed that nobody should deny us the right to take it. The vow of poverty, so central to a Franciscan understanding of discipleship, makes little sense in a world which seems obsessed with defining people by what they have. Choice extends into all areas of our lives. In some ways, we have more choice than ever before; as our access to information about the world has improved, so our horizons have broadened to include options we could not previously have considered. Yet the luxury of such choice is far from universal. Poverty and deprivation still divide the haves from the have-nots as absolutely as they did in the thirteenth century. The experience of poverty deprives people of more than money and things. People living in material poverty are also deprived of a voice, of energy, of hope that things will change. Poor people live shorter lives in poorer health, with inferior housing and limited opportunities. In the face of such inequality, where should the Franciscan honestly stand – with the very poor, or among those who have a chance to challenge the structures that ensure they stay that way?

The answer, perhaps, is both. Francis, after all, was concerned to acknowledge *every* creature as his brother or sister; both rich and poor could choose whether or not to listen to his message. Yet there is an especial Franciscan imperative to live and work alongside the truly poor, those whose poverty is a cause of pain and resentment rather than of freedom. Gospel living is about finding the means to bring about transformation in our own lives, and making the same possibility visible to others who need good news.

To be poor, sadly, is still to be without a voice and without power. In Francis' world, the poor were less than people. They could be bought, sold and discarded by those with the resources to choose. And they were expendable, easily replaced by someone else in the same plight. Arguably, 'the poor', wherever they are, are still less than people. The very phrase, 'the poor', lumps together and depersonalizes billions of individuals with different unique stories and voices which are seldom heard, because the rich and powerful shout more loudly.

It can be tempting for those attracted by Franciscan simplicity to rhapsodize about the ennobling properties of poverty. This is dangerously patronizing. It is important to understand that there is an essential difference between poverty as a chosen, life-giving option and the poverty which denies and dehumanizes. Living in unchosen poverty does not ennoble. Instead of freeing the mind from 'distractions' about food and clothes and other material concerns, they become an obsession. Far from being set free to live abundantly, this kind of poverty concentrates the mind on the mechanics of blind survival. And poor people are not necessarily any freer from materialism than the rich; they merely have less opportunity to indulge their desires. For the sake of clarity, then, it is necessary to draw a distinction between involuntary poverty, and a choice (or vocation) to live in simplicity in defiance of a world which defines us by what we have. Involuntary poverty, as experienced by billions of people worldwide, has no redeeming features. So much pious rhetoric about simplicity is, rightly, silenced by genuine need. Children starve and die because the food they need is kept from them by corrupt governments or power-hungry armies. Lives are blighted because of lack of access to health care or education. In such circumstances, it is utterly inadequate to speak of the life-giving joy to be found in a 'poverty' which millions of our brothers and sisters would see as unimaginable riches.

Of course there are, and always have been, many materially well-off people who refuse to be defined by possessions, wealth or status. However, it remains difficult to talk honestly about real poverty without some level of first-hand experience of its effects. Unless we are

willing to *become* poor, as Francis did, there will always
be a safety net of sorts to cushion us from life's more
brutal realities. Living a poor life, without the choice
which money and power can purchase, removes that
security. Few are willing to go to such literal lengths as
Francis and his early brothers. To live as one of the poorest in this country would involve life on the streets, shel-
tered by a cardboard box or a grubby sleeping bag. Yet
the poverty which Francis embraced in imitation of his
Master is of a different scale. It does not limit human
potential, in the way that the poverty we see on our tele-
visions or in our shop doorways does. Paradoxically, to
be poor in the way Francis was poor actually stretches
human potential, because it is no longer rooted in an
understanding which judges a person for what he or she
has. Extended beyond 'mere' money, the poverty of
Francis also refuses to limit people by what they can do.
Achievement, like money, birth or appearance, is essentially superficial. Franciscan poverty enables us to see
with the eyes of God – straight through to the heart.

The Little Poor Man

Francis' encounter with the leper on a mountain road
outside Assisi, as we have seen, was one of the defining
moments in the development of his particular vocation.
Francis' call to share God's love with the poorest began
with that unlikely embrace. When Francis first embraced
the leper, it was perhaps the first time he had encountered another person with nothing to hide. In the physically repulsive figure of the leper, Francis was confronted

with what he had been brought up to fear: powerlessness, absolute dependence, being nobody. Yet someone he would previously have avoided suddenly became a person to him. If one literally faceless nobody could embody Christ, there could be nothing for Francis to fear in letting go of the trappings that had previously shaped his identity. He was at last free to discover who he really was.

Francis was a product of his upbringing. It is hard to imagine someone poor from birth sharing his love affair with literal poverty and hardship. His obsession with not touching money verged on the pathological; there are stories of him forcing a brother who had touched coins to pick them out of a dungheap with his teeth, and his Rule is uncompromising: 'we should not think of coin or money having any greater usefulness than stones'.[1] This attitude is clearly bound up with his shame at his own previous excesses. For Francis was only too aware that being able to buy anything he wanted as a youth had kept him from experiencing life as it really was.

For Francis, though, a wholehearted pursuit of poverty meant more than just renouncing material wealth. He had grown up in the security of being a known, loved and wanted child. This experience enabled him to approach his heavenly Father with confidence, yet he had to reject his earthly family in order to give all of himself to God. Frances Teresa OSC has written of Francis' rejection of the values of his family as part of his struggle for a sense of self.[2] For a young man in his twenties, this is not at all unusual. In Francis, however, it went much deeper than a conventional refusal to work in the family business. His own dreams and assumptions about what it meant to be a person were bound up with being a Bernardone. When he publicly renounced his father, he was also renouncing himself; there was nothing left of the old Francis to define who he now was. In our own age, where identity and personality count for so much, such a gesture is almost beyond our scope to imagine. The attraction of being a somebody, first by virtue of his name and his social popularity and then through chivalry, was always strong. His insistence on being poor, little and lesser was a deliberate attempt to root out the temptation to return to the old life.

Despite the joy he found in following his Lord, Francis did not always find it easy to make the sacrifices required. One story recounts how he made a whole family for himself out of snow: wife, children and even servants, saying that this was the only family he would ever have. The pain of such loss is an inherent part of embracing all forms of poverty, voluntary or not. To accept poverty is to accept limitation.

Take No Thought for the Morrow

Francis' literal approach to poverty bordered at times on the extreme, even the unhealthy. His biographers remark admiringly that when he ate, he would add cold water or ashes to ensure that he did not enjoy the physical pleasure of eating.[3] This might seem inconsistent with his loving and positive approach to the things of creation. It is, however, consistent with his desire to be poor and little in every aspect of his life. Nobody was to be distressed by seeing Francis apparently subject to desires for the material. Instead, his example inspired many to repentance for the times they too had shut God out of their lives by clinging to objects, power and status.

In the terms understood by the rest of the world, and perhaps especially his father, Francis had deliberately chosen a material poverty that was beyond their comprehension. But he also saw the urgent need to become *spiritually* poor. Measured against the holy simplicity of Jesus Christ, he could only ever be little and insignificant. Francis must have been well aware that his behaviour would appear scandalous to many. The deliberate choice to be lesser, to become effectively a non-person, was not only an affront to his father's values. It was also a new theology.

Until Francis (and the Spaniard St Dominic, founder of the Order of Preachers) began to live as itinerant friars in the thirteenth century, men and women who wanted to live the religious life became monks or nuns. These usually lived under some form of the Rule of St Benedict in monasteries which were designed to supply all their needs, material and spiritual, thus cutting down the need for contact with the sinful values of the outside world. All distractions were removed so that the focus could be entirely on God. Benedict's emphasis on stability signifies a very different approach to that of the itinerant Franciscans: Benedictine monks and nuns are vowed to the particular house in which they live, and will expect to stay in one place until they die. Francis' understanding, by contrast, is that the world is our monastery. Everything in it belongs to God, rather than to us. We have no right to possess anything in it exclusively. We cannot take for granted that our needs will be met. For this reason, Francis maintained that his brothers should not eat unless they had worked or begged for their food. They were permitted to receive hospitality if it was freely offered, but if they begged and nobody gave them anything, they would go hungry.

In the Benedictine view, poverty is not a separate vow as it is for the Franciscan, but rather a constituent part of the distinctively Benedictine vow of *conversio morum* (conversion of manners). The possessions of the individual monk or nun are strictly regulated – everything they have for their use is in fact the property of the monastery in which they live. By Francis' time many monasteries were substantial landowners and employers. Though individual monks and nuns might have no more to call their own than a Franciscan brother or sister, they were likely to be able to draw on the considerable resources of an abbey foundation. The abbot or abbess had considerable power locally, and in the structures of the Church held rank equivalent to that of a bishop. This contrasts sharply with Francis' own insistence that none among the brothers should be called prior: 'Let one wash the feet of the other'.[4] Once again, his simplicity was revolutionary – although all he was doing was trying to emulate what Jesus had done.

Francis found in the poor those who could not choose to shield themselves from his message of love. Those who had nothing else they could use to give their lives meaning were those who most needed to hear that they were loved and valued by a God who does not work to human standards. In his insistence on becoming 'poor, yet making many rich',[5] Francis found that he was able to live more completely in imitation of Christ.

The insecure wandering lifestyle of the early Franciscan brothers is explicitly modelled on Jesus' commands to his disciples: Chapter Fourteen of the Earlier Rule ('How the Brothers Should Go Through the World') is studded with Gospel references. Such adherence to gospel values should be the goal of every Christian. However, when our identity and sense of self are bound up with what we have, it is easy to start justifying our 'need' to hang on to this or that object. If there is one passage of Scripture which sums up Franciscan simplicity, it is Luke 12: 22–34. The message could not be clearer; we are not to spend so much time worrying about *things*, or we will lose sight of the real treasure that is within our grasp. It seems so wonderfully simple, so uncluttered and focussed – yet so very hard to live.

That complete simplicity which costs no less than everything is not so attractive in day-to-day reality as it is in abstract. We look frantically for simplicity amidst the complications of modern existence, but we do not want to take on the limitations it will inevitably impose on our power to control our own lives. In our desperation to hang on to what we want, we forget God's promise to give us the things we truly need.

Poverty: a Challenge to the Church

Francis found companionship, and encouragement in his pursuit of poverty, in St Clare. Their shared love of

Poverty sustained and inspired them, and their brothers and sisters caught the infection. Like Francis, Clare was born to plenty. Her family was of a higher social class even than Francis', and it was expected that she would marry well to further their advantage. She was a woman, therefore not seen as a person in her own right in the eyes of either Church or secular law. The best she could hope for was to become a commercial commodity, to be used to further their social/economic standing.

But, like Francis, Clare was fiercely in love with God. As a teenager, she had been inspired by Francis' preaching. On the night of Palm Sunday 1212 she ran away to the brothers at the Portiuncola (Little Portion) outside Assisi. There she became the first Franciscan woman. Francis himself, it is said, cut off her hair, and replaced her clothes and jewellery with a rough tunic. From there, she was taken to a Benedictine community of nuns in Bastia, and eventually settled at San Damiano, the very place in which Francis had heard the crucifix calling him to rebuild the church. Other women, including members of her own family, soon came to join her, and the Poor Clares were born.

Theologians and biographers have argued about whether Clare would herself have preferred an itinerant lifestyle, similar to Francis', or whether she was truly called to the enclosed life of contemplation in which she spent over forty years. Whatever the truth, there can be no doubt either that she and Francis were closely bound together by their shared love of Christ, or that she shared his conviction about the absolute necessity of poverty.

Despite its enclosed monastic framework, the lifestyle

of Clare and her sisters was as poor as Francis' own. This posed a radical challenge to the Church's expectations of women. At that time it was not acceptable for women's orders to live in poverty. For well-born women, especially, it was considered scandalous to beg. Officially, they had to have some foundation, some resources on which to live. However, Clare resolutely rejected such expectations from outside. She was absolute in her insistence that she and her sisters would live in poverty, with nothing but what they received in alms. In 1216 the Pope granted Clare the 'Privilege of Poverty'; she and her Poor Ladies now had the right to live without the material safety cushions deemed appropriate for other women's communities. Yet the Clares lived for decades under rules written by other people; only in 1247 did they cease to be bound by the Rule of St Benedict, whose emphasis, as we have seen, was so fundamentally different to the Franciscan way. It was only shortly before her death in 1253 that the Pope finally granted recognition to Clare's own Rule, thus making her the first woman to write a rule for a women's community. There was no precedent for their particular way of life. Yet it caught on; women as well as men were eager to follow in the emergent way of Francis, and by Clare's death there were well over a hundred Poor Clare communities in Europe.

So what was it about Francis and Clare's insistence on poverty that was so apparently threatening for the Church? Their world saw status, power and the acquisition of wealth as a sign of God's favour. The theology of Francis and Clare turned that view on its head. The power and majesty of God had become entangled with the power of the institutional Church. They saw an urgent need for a return to gospel values, both for individual Christians and for the institution. The acquisition of land and power is exposed by Francis' preaching as worthless in God's scale of values. God is not glorified by possession, but by emptiness – only by becoming poor and dependent is the Church freed to become receptive.

However, Francis did not see his call to rebuild the Church as something destructive or rebellious. He was in awe of priests, those entrusted with the authority of God in the world. But Francis' own authority was considerable. It derived from authenticity and consistency of life, not from trappings. Authority was divorced from earthly power. All the gold and incense in the world could not convey the love of God to those who were poor as convincingly as the little poor man who preached from the gutter.

Lady Poverty

Francis' early ambition for success as a knight coloured his expression of his 'quest' for poverty. His discourse on his true love, Lady Poverty, ties in with the romantic troubadour songs of the period, which usually dealt with the unrequited love of a knight of low rank for an exalted lady. In the conventional traditions of the courtly love genre, the knight would never win the lady. She was so far above him as to be forever unattainable, but his heart would remain pure and his love true; his impossible love for the lady would inspire his feats on the battlefield. Such stories were the popular fiction of their day. Cruder versions did exist, in which the conventions were subverted by consummation of a love otherwise unthinkable. However, the majority not only coupled physical and spiritual purity, but also recognized the utter unworthiness of the one to possess the perfections of the other.

Such romantic conventions were part of the fabric of Francis' past. He desired 'Lady Poverty' with the true singlehearted passion of the troubadour knight. It could, however, be argued that he came to possess her and 'consummate' their relationship. *The Sacred Exchange Between St Francis and Lady Poverty*, in which their relationship is explored in depth by an unknown author, is a theological treatise which legitimizes the early friars' determination on a life of poverty. It offers a challenge to contemporary understanding of the monastic life, and a framework for a new approach. But it is also a love story. Francis, in imitation of his Lord who 'sought, found, and embraced' Poverty,[6] climbs the mountain where she lives, and through his relationship with her is brought ever closer to the God of all.

Poverty easily attracts a certain romanticism. As we have said, it is unlikely that someone born poor would have grasped poverty with such literal enthusiasm as Francis and Clare did. Yet the understanding of poverty and simplicity which they developed has a message for all of us, no matter what circumstances we were born into. There is no room in Franciscan living for false lyricism about the value of poverty for its own sake. The *Sacred Exchange* is scathing about those who pretend to be poor when they are not. Further, Lady Poverty is rejected and insulted by the poor who become rich; they use their new-found power to persecute the poverty they are now ashamed of. In doing so, they fail to realize that God is waiting for them in precisely the situation they are so eager to escape.

Francis and Clare have shown that there is a need for all thinking people to question whether any lasting worth can be found in pursuing material things. Experiences of vulnerability and loss cause us to go on asking such questions, to reassess the values by which we live and the identities we think we have chosen. The ideal of poverty, if it is not to remain an insubstantial romance, needs to be firmly rooted in experience. By becoming truly poor, we are equipped to share the pain of whole communities who feel abandoned and marginalized. It is in that experience of defenceless littleness that we really come to know the love of God. As Martin Luther was to point out in a Christmas sermon over three hundred years after Francis' death: 'We think of nothing but how to make ourselves high and well-regarded, not wanting God to see us in the depths, in our poverty, our weakness and our shame – the only place where he looks.'

Poverty, Chastity and Obedience

Religious life is often portrayed as an abnegation of responsibility, the refuge of the socially or emotionally inadequate from the demands of a confusing world. Who, given the choice, would turn from comfort and security in order to embrace a life of physical and material hardship, a life where ordinary satisfactions and consolations are permanently inaccessible? Yet this is exactly what Francis and Clare did, and exactly what their millions of followers have always tried to do in their own context.

Poverty as lived by Francis and Clare is not a picturesque 'lifestyle choice' for spoilt rich kids, but a deliberate imitation of the poverty of the crucified Christ, who had nothing to protect him from the harsh realities of his own humanity. The poor Christ on the cross who no longer does, but is done to – who has given away all and can only receive – is the logical extension of an incarnational theology which begins with the helpless infant God in the manger. The freedom to choose to die for us, the only freedom left in such poverty, paradoxically brings life in abundance. Such is the paradox of the vows; a death to self-determination brings unexpected joy and renewal.

Celano says of the brothers: 'Since they had nothing, they loved nothing; so they feared losing nothing.'[7] If even our life is seen as gift, not as our possession to be clung on to at all costs, we may perhaps be freed from the fear of death which so obsesses us. All of us, without exception, will one day have to embrace the ultimate vulnerability of death. No amount of money or power can shield us from that. Whatever we *can* afford to control, we have no way of paying anyone else to do it for us. Francis' devotion to absolute poverty shortened his life, but that would not have worried him – to die for love of Christ was, after all, what he desired.

The choice not to be limited by *things* is not restricted

to material poverty. All three of the Franciscan vows embody the same principle; to be freed from the limitations imposed on us by ownership and anxiety about the welfare of the things we have in our care or control. Chastity means that even my body is not my own, but at God's disposal – Francis' approach to Brother Ass, his body, demonstrates the same lack of possessiveness. The people with whom we live and work, those with whom we form any kind of relationship, are not ours to possess or control. Similarly, in this understanding of obedience, our own lives are handed over to God: 'not what I want, but what You want'.[8]

Poverty, chastity and obedience are no light option. Relinquishing control over our lives, and the choices to which we're used to thinking we have a right, is costly. Living under vows can teach us to cheat and evade their cost, or we can learn to take the risk to know ourselves as we most deeply are. Having nothing external by which to define ourselves, we are forced out of our hiding place. There is a radical freedom to be found in this kind of poverty: freedom from possessions, possessiveness and from being possessed. Francis found God in profound encounter with people, especially those in need. However, he also found it standing alone before God, the path between them uncluttered by obstacles or excuses.

What has love got to do with poverty? Francis' life says that it has everything to do with it. He was intent on living out the truth of Christ's incarnation: the Christ who was born poor and died poor in order to demonstrate the extent of God's love. Francis' own poverty

enabled him to become close to the most poor and out-
cast of his world, in order to make known to them the
hope and love always available in Christ. There were
to be no artificial barriers between his experience and
theirs. He could not cling to any advantage that made the
Gospel a comfortable option; poured out and emptied
like Jesus, he became a clearer mirror, in which ordinary
people saw their own chance to reflect God to the
world.

Love knows no limits. The limits imposed by the
structures and expectations of the world can be tran-
scended by love. The ideal of celibacy is a loving heart
which, claiming nobody exclusively for itself, can remain
free and available to all in need. In the choice to accept
dependence on God's will, the secret of chastity is also to
be found; a wholehearted, loving concentration on the
one relationship which gives meaning to all others.

Poverty of Spirit

Francis calls us not to flee from poverty, but to feel its
bite and limitations for ourselves. Life pared down to
basics, the absolute simplicity to which Francis aspired,
leaves nothing else to rely on but God. When you have
no possessions, no means to buy or bribe, reward or control the responses of other people, love is all you have at
your disposal. Francis knew that was enough for him –
he wanted nothing to keep him from the total embrace of
God.

Choice and power can be good; it is not wrong to want
such things. Where they begin to go wrong for us is when

we are able to use them to run away from the truth of who we are, or who we are called to be. Simplicity itself can also be falsely seductive, in that we can use it to avoid responsibility. It is important to acknowledge the truth that we are more than what we have. Yet to many, that very awareness is an unaffordable luxury. When what you have is not enough to pay the gas bill or buy shoes for the children, it is unrealistic to be expected to rise easily above that anxiety. It is then that the Franciscan imperative towards simplicity in right relationship comes into play: to become a resource for those who have exhausted their own resources and have nowhere else to turn. Simplicity is about becoming a resource for the world, not an exploiter of what it has to offer. It is not found in flight from the complexity of the material world and its claims on our energy and attention. Rather, it is met in engaging with those claims. Franciscan poverty brings us into relationship with those who have been bruised by their own experience of a dependence which they did not desire or choose.

Poverty of spirit is about knowing the true intrinsic value of things and their place in the order of creation, not about inflating the 'worth' of things unrealistically beyond what is in their power to give. This attitude robs money of the power with which it is usually invested. Clare and her aristocratic Poor Ladies rejoiced to have nothing but what they could beg; the brothers worked to eat, or else went without. Nothing was taken for granted as a commodity to which they had automatic right, nothing was exploited for their own gratification.

Poverty is about living with no masks, no props. In a

postmodern world it has become difficult to tell what really is, and what is illusion, effect, disguise, irony. Poverty can challenge all that. We find it desperately hard to live honestly, to confront ourselves as we really are. Remaining on the surface, we know we are missing out on something important, but the alternative is too risky to contemplate – the awareness of our own and others' utter vulnerability and dependence is as frightening as acknowledging our mortality. Yet in our very weakness and nakedness, we are better mirrors of Christ than the slick, successfully packaged myths we are sold with everything from soap powder to the Alpha course. A 'simplicity' which reduces everything to black and white by providing easily digestible answers is not the complete simplicity of Francis.

Poverty and Interdependence

Awareness of our dependence on God should flower into a sense of relatedness to our fellow creatures. In the face of poverty and injustice, one person can achieve little. This knowledge can paralyse us into total inaction, or it can stimulate us into reaching out to others who can help us look beyond our own limitations. A poverty which acknowledges our interdependence has great potential for a new understanding of what it means to be citizens of our world. Modern science scares us with its warnings of what will happen if we do not stop treating our environment as if it belonged to us to do as we like with. In Francis' ecology, we have no greater right to the world than other creatures; instead, we become resources for each other, sharing in the Creator's work of love and care for all that is.

Poverty, as we have seen, is not essentially to do with money. Most modern Franciscans are not poor by the world's standards. They have usually had to make some adjustments to the world in which they live: for example, it is not usually feasible to emulate Francis' literal poverty and refusal to touch money in cultures where begging is illegal. They have food and shelter, shared books and second-hand clothes; they can usually enjoy freedom of speech and of travel. Even in developing countries, they will probably have access to education and job opportunities which the majority of the population do not. True, by Western standards they are constrained by very limited resources. The modern Franciscan community may live in *simplicity*, but in most cases it is not the literal poverty of having nothing at all. Instead, the real poverty of community living tends to be that same poverty of choice. Frequent moves, never being able to put down roots; constantly having to renegotiate relationships; having to undertake uncongenial work or live with uncongenial people from whom there can be no escape; being constantly reminded of the call to look for our brothers and sisters in every creature.

Restriction of choice almost inevitably means a restriction of power; or at least of the power to dominate or buy one's way out of a situation. Even without financial power, it is still possible to choose to escape the cost of dependent gospel living: not by blatant refusal to live in the spirit of the vows, but through clinging to the more insidious 'comfort zones' which are quietly created in order to soften their impact. Overindulgence in food or drink, sleep or work, reading or emailing; the gradual creation of areas of personal power and influence; the development of cliques and exclusive relationships which contradict the principle that God's economy is built on the partnership of equals. But this is to avoid its reality – to diminish any attempt to live it fully. Exercising any kind of choice entails exercising responsibility. Poverty is about the mature choice not to use such escape routes, about being set free from being valued for what we have.

True Franciscan poverty can thus set us all free to live in right relationship with other people and with our world. Instead of the security which seals us off from one another in self-contained units, we can choose a simplicity which calls us together in mutual recognition. Not seeking to control, possess or dominate another, it becomes easier to accept the other as he or she is. There is no need to judge ourselves in comparison with someone else, or to despise ourselves if we are unable to attract or keep the objects of our desire. You are free to be you and I am free to be me. Thus we can live in a love which is innocent of power-games. God needs no other name, no label other than the one he gives to Moses: 'I AM what I AM'[9] – and, stripped of our destructive urge to possess and control, we are likewise enabled to be who we are. Without things or people against whom to measure our worth, the only remaining yardstick is God.

Suggested Exercises

1. Recall an episode when you felt powerless. How did you feel? How did you cope with the experience? Be objective, not judging yourself. You may find it helpful to write or draw as you reflect. Talk to God about it.

2. If you are able, set aside several hours to go for a long walk; don't take money or anything else with you, but concentrate only on what you are doing. Notice your surroundings – sights, sounds, smells, people and objects. Notice your mood; don't censor thoughts or feelings but let them surface. If it helps, imagine that Jesus is walking with you. What do you want to say to him, to confide or share? Does he have things to say to *you*?

5

Song of Creation

Most High, all-powerful, good Lord,
Yours are the praises, the glory, and the honour, and
  all blessing,
To You alone, Most High, do they belong,
and no human is worthy to mention Your name.
Praised be You, my Lord, with all Your creatures,
Especially Sir Brother Sun,
Who is the day and through whom you give us light.
And he is beautiful and radiant with great splendour;
And bears a likeness of You, Most High One.
Praised be You, my Lord, through Sister Moon and
  the stars,
In heaven you formed them clear and precious and
  beautiful.
Praised be You, my Lord, through Brother Wind,
And through the air, cloudy and serene, and every
  kind of weather,
Through whom You give sustenance to Your
  creatures.
Praised be You, my Lord, through Sister Water,
Who is very useful and humble and precious and
  chaste.
Praised be You, my Lord, through Brother Fire,
Through whom You light the night,
And he is beautiful and playful and robust and strong.

Praised be You, my Lord, through our Sister Mother
   Earth,
Who sustains and governs us,
And who produces various fruit with coloured flowers
   and herbs.
Praised be You, my Lord, through those who give
   pardon for Your love,
And bear infirmity and tribulation.
Blessed are those who endure in peace
For by You, Most High, shall they be crowned.
Praised be You, my Lord, through our Sister Bodily
   Death,
From whom no one living can escape.
Woe to those who die in mortal sin.
Blessed are those whom death will find in Your most
   holy will,
For the second death shall do them no harm.
Praise and bless my Lord and give him thanks
And serve him with great humility.

(St Francis, *Canticle of the Creatures*)[1]

The *Canticle of the Creatures*, or the Canticle of Brother Sun, is the most famous of the writings of St Francis. One of the earliest existing poems in medieval Italian, it is familiar to many Christians in the form of the hymn 'All creatures of our God and King'. Reading the joyful and celebratory words of the Canticle, it is easy to forget that it was in fact written not long before Francis' death, at a time of great physical and emotional suffering. He had been severely afflicted by a disease of the eyes, and the depredations to which 'Brother Ass' had been subjected for many years were taking their toll in increasing physical debility. Furthermore, divisions and factions were beginning to show up in the Order itself, causing great distress to Francis. Yet the *Canticle of the Creatures* is a great affirmation of faith and hope. Through the Canticle we can gain a greater understanding of Francis' approach to theology, and to the world which communicated God to him at every turn.

The Crown of Creation?

Francis' Canticle, with its assumption that all created things are linked in brotherhood under God, presents an apparent challenge to the anthropocentric view of the universe. Francis' assertion of brotherhood, relatedness, with every creature, is shocking to us because we have been affected by the Enlightenment assumption that our human ability to think and reason makes us the pinnacle of creation. In this view, the role of God as the Creator is easily sidelined, and human beings assume a central role. Humans stand at the top of the hierarchy not because they have souls which mirror God more perfectly than any other creature can, but because they have the intelligence to dominate and alter their environment to suit themselves. Similarly, there is an assumption that the place of human beings in the created order gives them the right to do as they will with other creatures. In Genesis, all the animals and plants are given into Adam's care, and he also has the responsibility for giving them their names: an important role which speaks of recognition of their essence. Finding the right name means acknowledging and celebrating the uniqueness of each creature. However, Genesis goes on to chronicle how human beings presumed too much on their unique degree of relationship with God. The view that every creature is made to honour and praise God by the very fact of their being was soon over-ridden by an assumption of humans' right to dominate and control those around them. In the vision of the Psalmist, too, there is an uneasy balance. Here, a humble recognition that human beings are God's creatures like any other seems to contrast with glorying in their 'mastery' over other beings:

> What are mortals, that you should be mindful of
> them?
> mere human beings, that you should seek them out?
> You have made them little lower than the angels;
> you adorn them with glory and honour.
> You give them mastery over the works of your hands;
> and put all things under their feet,
> all sheep and oxen,
> even the wild beasts of the field,
> the birds of the air, the fish of the sea,
> and whatsoever walks in the paths of the sea.[2]

As the story of the wolf of Gubbio makes explicit, Francis shared the view that human beings were the crown of God's creation. He reproved the wolf for attacking people on the specific grounds that they are made particularly in the image of God. It was in human form that God chose to be born into the world. Humans have souls, and the potential for eternal life should they choose it; other creatures do not. In this view, Francis was no different from the majority of Christian theologians. Humans were indeed perceived as 'little less than the angels', and other creatures took their places below them in the 'natural order' of the universe. However, the Canticle also makes clear that Francis' particular vision of creation was not limited to a hierarchy with humanity at the top. Rather, it seems to suggest that creation is based on a relationship of equals, with God as the summit and the focus of all he had made. 'Sir Brother Sun', we are told, bears the likeness of God, and all his creatures likewise are living signposts to the Creator in their own way; the characteristics of each reflect God back to the world in a particular and distinctive way which is theirs alone.

Human beings need to remember that our special status as creatures with souls does not make us the centre of the universe. We have, perhaps, become so aware of our own potential for power over our environment, our increased ability to push back the boundaries of the unknown and inexplicable, that we have lost any sense of ourselves as creatures. In the light of so much great human achievement and progress, it is tempting to believe that we have created and determined ourselves. Francis' Canticle reminds us that we do not possess such a right. Human beings are indeed the pinnacle of creation, because of their status as the creature which most closely resembles the Creator, but they still fall short of the glory of God. If humans are to find our rightful place within the pattern of creation and live in healthy relationship with the rest of the creatures of the universe, it is in rediscovering our intended role as God's stewards; not given the right of dominance over the rest of creation, but responsibility for its care on God's behalf. As the creatures who most closely correspond to the pattern of the Maker of all, human beings need to treat other species with the same loving respect, concern and desire for well-being that went into the creation of each.

The Divine Economy

As we have previously acknowledged, Francis was in no way sentimental about animals – though some of the stories about him do lend themselves to such an interpretation. In Thomas of Celano's *Life of St Francis*, he describes how the saint loved even the humblest of creatures; for example, he would pick up worms and move them to the side of the road to avoid their being trodden on. Bees, too, inspired Francis to love and admiration; he would make sure that they were fed during the winter months so that the cold did them no harm, and in summer could spend long periods in contemplation of 'the artistry of their work and their remarkable ingenuity'.[3] However, Celano makes it clear that such devotion, even to the smallest representatives of the creation, stemmed directly from Francis' overpowering love for God. When Francis owned all creatures as his brothers and sisters it was because he had an unusual ability to 'discern the secrets of the hearts of creatures',[4] the secrets of their being given to them by the Creator. In so discerning, he was able to find in each one the potential to glorify God. In this recognition of their own essential qualities, other creatures are thus set free to glorify the Creator by being themselves. The story of the wolf of Gubbio emphasizes that this process does not require animals to become anthropomorphized. Instead, any attempt to discover the secrets of the heart of another creature will force humans to recognize their differing needs – and the responsibility of stewards to see that those needs are appropriately met.

Stewardship correctly exercised on behalf of the Creator, as we have seen, means that humans have no right to exercise power and control over animals, plants, minerals or elements. Today, we understand much more about the complex networks of interdependence between species in our ecosystem. We are beginning, too, to understand more of the dangers inherent in altering the balance of that ecosystem. In Francis' view of the divine economy of creation, all creatures are to live together in mutuality, without exploitation or abuse.

His own relationship with the creatures of the earth can seem devastatingly matter-of-fact. For example, a sow that killed a lamb was cursed;[5] though this seems uncharacteristic of Francis, it may be taken in the same spirit as Jesus' cursing of the fig tree[6] which had also ceased to behave in a way appropriate to its kind. One of the most popular Francis stories depicted in art or statuary is the occasion on which he preached to the birds – but what he said to them is much less well known. Celano reports that, echoing Jesus' words about the lilies of the field, Francis exhorted them to praise their Creator who had given them 'feathers to wear, wings to fly, and whatever you need',[7] although they did no work to deserve it. It is further explained that his desire to preach to animals and birds as well as people was prompted by observing their obedience. Once, trying to preach at a place called Alviano, he could not be heard because of the noise of swallows who were nesting in the nearby woods. Addressing them as his sisters, Francis asked the swallows to be quiet until he had finished speaking, so that the word of the Lord should not be interrupted; to general amazement the swallows remained still and silent for the duration of the sermon. Thus it is evident that Francis' attitude to animals and birds was neither sentimental nor indulgent. He loved them as fellow creatures of the one God, and wanted them to know of the reality of God's love for them. He merely expected to find in them the same reverence for their Lord and Creator as he wanted to instil in human beings. The reaction of the various creatures he encountered suggests that, through the reality of love in action, it is always possible to transform behaviour and call out untapped potential.

Acknowledging a relationship with all creatures as equals in God's sight borders on the revolutionary. To insist on being brother to the worm is to take poverty and littleness to its logical conclusion. To call fire and water our brother and sister is to claim kinship with some of the most ungovernable forces on the planet. In the theology of Francis' Canticle they are no longer strange and alien, but through recognition of our shared status as God's creatures we come to inhabit our natural environment in a more honest way. Our brother fire is no longer to be feared as an enemy, or worshipped as a god in the hope that it will not consume us, but can warm and delight us. However, in order to do so, it requires us to feed it and tend it. Thus the other creatures become our partners in the journey of life. As with literal brothers and sisters, our relationship can be a harmonious and fruitful one, or it can be destructive and diminishing. In the vision of the Canticle, we are prompted to recognize our common vocation of praising God through being what we were created to be. The highest purpose of any creature, however simple or complex, is to honour the God who made it. Seen all together, the characteristics of all the creatures named in the Canticle (beauty, radiance, splendour, chastity, purity, serenity, strength, and so on) help us to build up a picture of their Creator. Each creature, however insignificant, can tell us something about the mind that called it into being.

Human development is a process of gradual assimilation, of coming to terms with oneself as one is and the world as it is. The mature human being needs to move beyond preoccupation with the self and the individual world view, into an eventual position of acceptance of the validity of other views and ways of being. When extended beyond humans to include *all* creatures, this presents an important ecological challenge – a true relationship of equal partners, which is respectful of other creatures' needs and otherness, cannot be based in greed and desire for control. Instead, it needs to be rooted in love and humility, as humans begin to tease out

appropriate ways to live in a world to whose vulnerability they have unwittingly contributed. Human beings,
the most nearly Godlike of all creatures, now have
to take seriously their role as stewards of the earth.
Enabling all God's creatures to live to their full potential,
as each was created to do, is to assist in the ongoing work
of creation.

Embracing Sister Death

Being aware of ourselves as creatures will often entail
awareness of how far we have fallen short of the ideal
which is represented by God who made us in his image.
As the *Common Worship* communion liturgy puts it: 'we
have wounded your love and and marred your image in
us'. Thinking of ourselves as creatures is not necessarily
a comfortable process. To accept that we are creatures is
to acknowledge a degree of dependence which is not
comfortable in the light of our modern insistence on self-
determination. Yet the fact is that dependence is pro-
grammed into us. Human infants remain helpless longer
than the young of any other species. And however
powerful we may become in worldly terms, we are
inevitably going to die.

　　In the midst of its celebration of creation, the *Canticle
of the Creatures* does not shy away from the reality
of death. On the contrary, Francis' words encourage
a proper preparation for the inevitable. The role of
penance in that preparation will be examined more
closely in Chapter 7. Death for Francis was the ultimate
joy – *that undiscovered country from whose bourn no*

traveller returns[8] was for him the place of uninterrupted and perfect union with a loving God, as promised at the end of Romans 8. Francis never shied from the harsher realities of existence. Pain and death are thus embraced in the Canticle as part of the human experience through which we are called to return to our Creator.

Acknowledging death as a sister, as just another of God's creations, enables it to take its rightful place as part of the pattern of life. In Francis' understanding, it is to be welcomed and celebrated as a step to something greater. To claim kinship with death, as with fire or water, is to rob it of some of the 'otherness' which might otherwise breed fear and alienation. Just as the other creatures in the Canticle tell us something important about God and how we can relate to him, so too does Sister Death. The fact that God himself did not choose to remain immune from death is immensely important in understanding the relationship he wants with us, the creatures made in his image. In order that *every* human experience, without exception, might be able to draw us closer to him, God must enter into every aspect of our existence, including its end.

Some Christian churches are uncomfortable with displaying the crucifix. They do not like to dwell on the pain and death of Jesus on the cross; after Easter, they say, there is no need to think about that aspect. He died, yes, but we are assured that he lives for ever, so there is no point in making ourselves uncomfortable by thinking morbid thoughts. However, human beings have a great need for a spirituality which can be honest about death.

The context in which Francis lived meant that most

people did not have the luxury of prolonged life expectancy and good health care. In many of the world's poorest countries, for the same reasons, there is still no room for sentimentality about death. Life expectancy for millions is still lower than the 44 years that Francis managed. Babies and children routinely die for lack of appropriate medical care and nourishment. Women still die in childbirth. Wars and violence born out of frustration claim millions of lives. In the West, by contrast, death still seems to be the great unmentionable. It has become so much more possible to avoid facing the reality of death. Advances in science and medicine have meant that it is easier to believe we can keep it at bay. Many conditions that used to be fatal are now easily treatable. Even wars tend to happen elsewhere.

We have got so used to being in control, of harnessing our power over so much of nature, that death seems an affront rather than a natural conclusion. Disasters make us feel vulnerable in our sudden, unwelcome awareness of our own mortality. One of the shocks of the 11 September attacks and their aftermath was the assault on the sense of invulnerability which had, without our being aware of it, taken deep root in much of the industrialized West. 'I never thought this would happen to me', became the cry of millions, forgetting that countless others, never having known what it is to have power over their own lives, have never had the luxury of assuming themselves immune.

Most of us would want to believe that we value life. Yet what we value most, perhaps, is *not being dead*. It is difficult to imagine that there will ever come a time when we will not be there any more, not able to control our surroundings or to communicate our uniqueness. Even in our supposedly secular age, opinion polls consistently show that many people who would not consider themselves conventionally religious still profess a belief in some kind of afterlife. Death, then, is not necessarily the end. Francis was absolutely clear that it was nothing of the sort. On the contrary, it was for him a gateway to a new stage of life in Christ, who himself had passed through death to new life. Despite their grief, the brothers rejoiced at Francis' death because of their love for him.

According to the Canticle, those who have lived in obedience to God have nothing to fear, either this side of the grave or beyond it. Sister Death herself welcomes them on their journey out of this life, and the judgement which lies ahead holds no terrors for the righteous, for 'the second death will do them no harm'. In Francis' joyful Canticle there is hope in every relationship and every experience. Suffering and death, rather than obscuring the way to God, prepare the soul for the real adventure of union with him.

Power and Poverty

The *Canticle of the Creatures* inspires us to follow St Francis in building equitable relationships, creating a sense of community with the other creatures who inhabit the world. This grandiose-sounding aim is intensely difficult to live out. Francis' own literal following of Christ led him to discover that he was called to echo the prayer of Jesus in Gethsemane: 'Not what I will, but what You will'.[9]

Terrorism is usually born out of a relationship between poverty, or choicelessness, and power. People who feel they know intimately what it feels like to be violated and voiceless seize power over others in order to make their point. It has been said that suicide bombers, for example, use themselves as a weapon because it is all that they have. Taking control of your own death is seen as preferable to being passive and waiting to be killed by someone else. It is, in the final reckoning, a way of making sure of being noticed when no other means have worked. Some may take this most extreme form of protest out of a misguided sense that by doing so they will become martyrs for their cause. However, it is arguable that it is not possible, theologically speaking, to martyr yourself; martyrdom is something which can only be done *to* you. Francis was asked if he would prefer to endure martyrdom than to suffer from the illness which dominated his last years. He replied that he desired only to do whatever was more pleasing to God. To suffer his illness for only three days, he said, would be harder for him than to be martyred; but that, in the end, was the particular voice which his poverty found.

Power, like choice, is not bad in itself. As the *Canticle of the Creatures* reminds us, humans are given almost unlimited power by God to choose the manner in which they will live. They can choose the abuse or manipulation of that power over other creatures, or they can opt to live in right relationship, learning to recognize and value their brothers and sisters as precious in God's sight and their own.

At the service of profession of vows in a religious community, the candidate is asked: 'Do you make these vows of your own free will?' The only honest answer to that, for many, is *no*. Many religious would say that when they made the vows of poverty, chastity and obedience, it was because they knew it was right, and that it was what they believed God was calling them to do – but they might not necessarily feel that there was any real choice. The words of Luther: '*Here I stand, I can do no other*', are resonant of this relationship between choice and powerlessness, where the *only* choice about how to live is to accept or refuse what they know to be right. For Francis and Clare, too, there was only one way of integrity. Obedience was central to their lives. Nobody *ordered* them to give up affluence and security in order to follow the gospel. Many have been able to listen and respond to the promptings of God without going to such extremes. They could have said no. Yet if they were so sure of what God required of them, would they have felt they had any choice? Christian obedience is about taking a fair share of responsibility, being accountable for one's own actions. Even where an individual brother or sister cannot agree with the direction the community seems to be taking or with decisions it has made, there is a responsibility to the rest of the community to contribute towards making it work. The mind of the community is greater than what any individual might desire or perceive to be right for them. There is not one set of needs or perspectives to be considered in reaching that mind, but many. Such questions mirror the preoccupations of any human grouping about how to balance power and respect.

All three of the traditional Franciscan vows are under-pinned by living in right relationship with power and choice. Poverty, or freedom from possessions, entails the renunciation of power over things; chastity, the freedom to give oneself singleheartedly to God, requires the renunciation of power over others; and most demand-ingly of all, obedience offers freedom through the renun-ciation of power over one's own will. In essence, all the vows are about making a choice not to *have* choice; aligning oneself with the voiceless and powerless in a way that is intended, paradoxically, to be life-giving. The vows can seem pointless. They can, if lived less than wholeheartedly, become dry and mean, life-denying and crippling. That is not love at work, but fear; the fear of being vulnerable enough to let God in. In God's presence the vows offer freedom to do the unexpected. Like Francis' extremes, their shock value can repel – or it can cause others to reassess their own lives.

The whole of the *Canticle of the Creatures*, with its insistence on mutually beneficial interdependence and loving respect, is also shot through with the ideals of poverty, chastity and obedience. All humanity, not just those bound by religious vows, needs to learn the art of living in responsible, non-possessive, non-exploitative partnership. Every creature must eventually come to terms with its need for and dependence on God. The Canticle holds out to each one the possibility of being loved as God loves – for who we are, or at least could be.

Suggested Exercises

1. You might like to write or draw your own version of the Canticle. What are the things for which you most want to praise God?

2. Francis was able to praise God for everything that surrounded him; he perceived God not just in the natural world, but at work in every aspect of life. Study an everyday object closely. Consider the work which has gone into its design and construction. Notice how any signs of wear, neglect and repair have contributed to its character. Reflect on the same process of change and creativity at work in your own life. Psalm 139 may help you to focus on this.

6

Obedience

What you hold, may you always hold.
What you do, may you always do and never abandon.
But with swift pace, light step, and unswerving feet,
so that even your steps stir up no dust,
go forward securely, joyfully, and swiftly,
on the path of prudent happiness,
believing nothing,
agreeing with nothing
which would dissuade you from this resolution
or which would place a stumbling block for you on the
*   way,*
so that you may offer your vows to the Most High
in the pursuit of that perfection
to which the Spirit of the Lord has called you.

(St Clare, *Second Letter to Blessed Agnes of Prague*)[1]

Holy Listening

Which is the most difficult of the three vows by which
Francis lived? Chastity may seem less a way to freedom
of the heart than a cowardly or arid renunciation of the
risks inherent in loving and being loved. Poverty, likewise, may offer only anxiety instead of the intended

freedom from attachments. Yet, of the three, it is the idea of obedience that tends to get the strongest negative reaction.

In a world which appears to prize above all the fulfilment of the individual, obedience is a difficult concept to take seriously. Why should anyone live in subjection to the will of another? Why would anyone choose to do so, if they didn't have to? In Rumer Godden's famous novel about life in a Benedictine monastery, *In This House Of Brede*, one of the nuns comments that if anyone had told her before she joined that she would have to give up her will to another, she would rather have been shot. Such questions are not restricted to religious obedience. Public confidence in *any* institution which has been used to wielding authority over the way people live their lives – politics, the law, the Church – has been irrevocably dented, if not completely lost.

Such a loss of confidence is perhaps rooted in confusion about the proper relationship between obedience, authority, rights and power. Where respect for an institution has been lost, it can usually be traced back to an inappropriate assumption on the part of that institution of the way to use power, or perhaps even of the right to wield it at all. The Latin derivation of the word 'obedience' itself suggests that to equate it with slavish submission or the misuse of power is a mistake. True obedience is instead rooted in listening, an act which can only take place in relationship. It is not about compliance, power wielded by one over another. Nor is it to be assumed that obedience will be automatic. Instead, we deal with obedience here under the heading of Love because obedience, being about listening and communicating, mutual attentiveness and respect, lies at the heart of loving relationships. The problem that many women have had with the promise to obey, as it was set out in the old marriage service, was that when only one partner has to promise to listen to the other, there is an instant imbalance. All of us need to feel that we have been heard, and a healthy relationship will be difficult if that mutuality is absent. The same is true in every area of life.

The Christian gospel shows how this perspective on obedience might work. Obedience, in the religious sense, is not to be equated with an unhealthy submission to a despotic God who moves human pieces around the chessboard of creation. Listening, through prayer and through learning to distinguish God at work in the suggestions or advice of others, is again central. Hearing – or, to use religious jargon, discerning – what God is asking is a difficult art. It can be so tempting to imagine God is asking something of us because it seems right and comfortable; what is really being asked may be much less immediately attractive.

Yet, where the will has been coerced and power used inappropriately, there is no true obedience. Rather, its meaning is uncovered through a gradual process of discernment of God's will. Even God does not force us to do what we do not want to do. His power is at our disposal, to enable us perhaps to do what we might not otherwise feel able to attempt, but it will not be wielded over us. God waits for us to choose the right thing to do *because we want to*; as we discern his will, our own grows towards alignment with it, yet without jeopardizing our prized autonomy as human beings.

Francis and Obedience

For the religious person, obedience to God comes first. Thus it may override a sense of obligation to any institution of human origin. Francis' Rule and *Testament* tell us a lot about his own approach to obedience, within the framework of that understanding. God's will is paramount. Only by uncovering it and trying to live by it do we really come to understand our own deepest desire.

From his writings, it would seem that Francis' ideas about obedience and authority evolved as the community grew up around him – and then again as he stepped aside from a position of leadership, handing on the day-to-day running of a newly established community that needed regulation. He too was born in a time that questioned established institutions and patterns of authority. The townspeople of Assisi had turned against hereditary rulers some years before, and established government by commune. The Church, too, was coming under question because of its fascination with power and wealth. This sometimes made for a complex relationship between the Little Brothers and the ecclesial structures, which will be examined further in Chapter 7.

In his *Letter to a Minister*, Francis connects true obedience with the command to love one another, even – perhaps especially – those whom it is difficult to like. In this way Francis acknowledges the human reality of community life, but points a way forward to the ideal:

an atmosphere of mutual accountability, where all contribute to discerning the mind of the whole community,
and all (including those in positions of leadership) are
bound by the decisions which express that common
mind. The different foci of obedience – God, the person
in charge, the community as a whole – should not be in
conflict with each other, but run parallel, so that each
person's obedience to the will of the community stems
from a common desire to do the will of God.

'What could be more hopeless than a religious who
despises obedience?' asks the *Assisi Compilation*. This
collection of stories, seemingly put together by some of
the early brothers who had known Francis at first hand,
gives more detail of how Francis approached relationships in community. It begins with remarks about his
attitude to obedience, stressing that despite its importance, he never saw it as something to be forced: 'The
weapon of last resort should not be the first one used.'[2]
The brothers, whatever their personal differences, are
bound together by a shared love of God. Those in
authority stand in the place of God, and are to be rever-
enced by the brother who finds himself under obedience
'for the love of Whom he is subject'.[3] The authority held
by ministers and other leaders is not to be used for their
own aggrandizement, but is a gift of God, made available
for the whole community. Authority and power are thus
the servants of all the brothers, rather than their masters.

When the time came for him to step down, Francis
declared himself obedient not just to God but to those
now in authority in the community, and he commended
the same model of obedience to all his brothers. Francis

did not cling on to leadership, or the power and status which attend it. In the monastic model, by contrast, an abbot was usually elected for life, retaining absolute power over every aspect of the community. The position of a founder who is no longer in day-to-day control of his foundation, but still living as part of it, can become troublesome for those who take it on. Similarly, it has proved problematic for many to disentangle the moral or spiritual authority vested in a *person* from that pertaining to the position they hold. The *Letter to a Minister* makes it clear that Francis was aware of some of these potential difficulties. The delicate balance of power and responsibility in a community setting could only hold if all concerned were willing to love and to listen to each other.

Francis also stressed that some matters of obedience must be left to the individual conscience, recognizing that there may be times at which it may actually be inappropriate to obey orders from the hierarchy. Obedience to the Rule and those who administer it is *part*, but not the whole, of the members' obedience to God – and if the community or its leaders diverge from the will of God, it is God who must command the greater loyalty. The contemporary *Principles* of the Society of Saint Francis similarly recognize that 'none may, on any authority, act contrary to the guiding of their own consciences'.[4] There must always be room for that ongoing process of discerning the will of God, both for the individual and the community – and openness to the Holy Spirit often brings surprises!

Death to Self

The concept of death to self was central to Francis' understanding of obedience. The idea crops up several times in the writings of both Francis and Clare. It was especially potent for Francis. Only by dying to the old life – symbolized both by the time he spent hiding from his father in a pit near San Damiano, and then in the public stripping off of his identity in court – could he be free to start the new. Like conversion, though, it was a continuing process.

Death to self underlay the old life profession ceremony in many religious communities. The candidate would lie prostrate on the floor in front of the altar, covered by a pall, as if actually dead; when he or she arose, it was to a new 'perfected' self. The past was forgotten; from now on the newly professed would have no identity, nothing of their own to keep God at bay. The whole self had been handed over completely to God, so that 'it is no longer I who live, but Christ who lives in me'.[5] Dying to self, as Francis and Clare understood it, led them into deeper relationship with the Christ for whom they now lived.

Does obedience *require* this kind of death to self? Such emphasis carries considerable risks. Stories abound of religious made ill by a too literal pursuit of the ideal. Forced to abandon aspects of self which they actually needed in order to function as mature human beings, they were unable to grasp that death to self makes sense only if it is not the end of a process, but the gateway to something new and abundantly alive. Francis explicitly likened his own obedience to God to that of a corpse –

the dead body, stripped of all volition, can do nothing of itself, but can only be done to. In his book *The Stature of Waiting*,[6] W. H. Vanstone shows how Christ undergoes a similar process in the passion narrative in Mark's Gospel. Passivity and passion are powerfully linked: the very process of dying results, mysteriously, in new life.

Your Will Be Done

Francis' 'Prayer inspired by the Our Father' expressed his singlehearted desire to live the life to which God was calling him. The 'Our Father' itself reminds us once again of the mutual relationship which underpins prayer. Religious people pray because they believe God is listening. God listens to prayer out of love for those whom he has created. So, too, Jesus taught his own disciples to say 'Your will be done' as an essential expression of their relationship with God their Father. Francis' reflections were offered out of his belief that there is literally nothing better we can do to express our own love than the will of our Creator:

> *Your will be done on earth as in heaven*
> That we may love You
> With our whole heart by always thinking of You
> With our whole soul by always desiring You,
> With our whole mind by always directing all our
>   intentions to You
> and by seeking Your glory in everything,
> With all our whole strength by exerting

all our energies and affections of body and soul
in the service of Your love and of nothing else . . .[7]

Praying the Our Father obediently can be an experience
of terrifying power; 'Your will be done' is perhaps the
most dangerous thing anyone can ask of God. Having
taught his disciples to pray in those very words, Jesus
himself was to pray them, painfully, on the night before
his death. Knowing he could still pray to escape that
death and be answered, instead he chose to do his
Father's will. His divine power is set aside as he listens to
the needs of his people, cementing his loving relationship
with them by being willing to die for them.

Francis too, the deacon, the least and the servant of all
his brothers, modelled himself on the self-emptying
Christ who was 'obedient to death, even death on a
cross'.[8] The desire to die to self and live to Christ was
eventually given visible expression in Francis' own
body. Two years before he died, while praying all night
on Mount Alverna, he received the stigmata, the five
wounds of the Crucified. In this way Francis came to live
the very meaning of passion, of being 'done to' by God.
His obedient stripping and emptying of self, like Christ's
own, was born of a love which desired only union with
the Beloved. Such love, such passion, left nothing but a
space to be filled utterly with God.

Fear of being asked to die to self and give up a
cherished picture of the future, perhaps of losing one's
identity altogether, is a common response to God's call.
How can I do the will of God, become more truly the
image of God, and yet remain myself? St Catherine of
Genoa offers a solution: 'My me *is* God; nor do I find my

selfhood except in him.' In such a view, obedience becomes a way to perfect freedom; to obey God by letting go of self is not to diminish that self, but to find it for the first time.

Obedience and Vocation

If prayer is an expression of mutual love and commitment, then as well as the loving God listening to the petitions of his people, it is incumbent upon those same people to work at their side of the relationship by listening for God's word and acting on it. Francis and Clare encouraged their brothers and sisters to be especially attentive to that word as expressed in Scripture. Francis' Rule of 1221, for example, explicitly says that true obedience is to be found when a brother keeps God's commandments according to the gospel. 'Love one another as I have loved you,' one of Jesus' few direct commandments to his disciples, is the blueprint for religious obedience. It is one model of Christian witness to which all are called, regardless of circumstance, gift or preference.

A glance at the Bible, though, confirms that the initial response of many prophetic figures to their own particular calling from God was far from singlehearted obedience. A variety of excuses are initially proffered for being unable to do what God is asking. Moses says he cannot speak in public in a way that will convince the Israelites; Jeremiah claims to be too young; Jonah tries to evade his commission altogether. God has to come up with a range of signs and wonders to convince each of them that they will not be left alone with their daunting new tasks. His presence, his commitment to a relationship of mutual attentiveness, will strengthen and encourage them as they fulfil their vocation.

By contrast, Francis never seems to have hesitated or argued with God about the direction his life was taking. Listening to God perfectly, with every aspect of one's being, silences one's own inner protests and reservations. For Francis, then, obedience was expressed in immediate action on the promptings of the Spirit. Sure that he *had* heard God's voice, he was ready to do what was asked of him. Clare, too, describes in her *Testament* how her own sense of vocation came direct from God, leading her and her first sisters to 'offer voluntary obedience' to Francis, whose calling complemented her own. For both, once the will of God had been recognized and accepted, there could be no deviation from working to fulfil it.

The language of vocation, however, is not restricted to the 'professionally' religious. Clare's *Testament* explains how she wanted her sisters to be a mirror and example for those around them of the kind of life which was possible in God. Nobody is excluded from realizing that possibility. Saints are not special people in that they are equipped any differently from the rest of the human race. What marks them out is the quality, if not always the immediacy, of their response to God. Emulating a saint might be as unthinkable to the average person as emulating a serial killer. However, each individual has the potential to develop for good or ill, to discover their own particular vocation or calling to reflect God in a unique way. The popularity of Francis and Clare has inspired many ordinary people to consider their own response to a God whose call may become audible at any time, not least through existing networks of human relationship.

Responsible Listening

The various conversion experiences of Francis' life reflect an inner growth towards deeper attentiveness, culminating eventually in total union with God. Obedience, in the sense of this kind of attentive listening, brings us still closer into relationship. Where that relationship is damaged or compromised, so too is the ability to listen and respond openly. Listening, as we have said, has to go hand in hand with discernment as to the appropriate response. Obedience to something bigger and stronger than ourselves, for example, can be motivated solely by fear and the wish to propitiate, which have nothing to do with loving mutuality.

It is possible to take a coherent view of Franciscan obedience only within the context of Francis' primary desire to have, or to be, nothing other than what God desired for him. Even seen in this light, his demands on his brothers could occasionally seem exaggerated, even verging on the ridiculous. A fourteenth-century biographer, Bartholomew of Pisa, recounts the story of two aspirants to the order, who were asked to copy Francis exactly. He then proceeded to plant a row of cabbages upside down, telling the aspirants to do the same. One did so, but the other questioned him, pointing out that cabbages do not grow with leaves in the ground and roots in the air. Francis' response was terse: 'I see that you are very learned, but you will not do for my Order.'[9]

In seeking to understand Franciscan obedience, there is an important distinction to be drawn between the child*like* pursuit of simplicity and the child*ish* abrogation of responsibility. Jesus himself extols a childlike open-mindedness to his disciples; several of Francis' biographers praise his childlike playfulness, innocence and wonder. These qualities freed him to take risks in pursuit of a deepening relationship with God. Others' attempts to emulate such singleheartedness, however, were not always appreciated by those, including Francis himself, who had to pick up the pieces. The irrepressibly simple Brother Juniper is the most telling example. In one famous story, Juniper asked a sick brother if there was anything he would like to eat. The brother asked for a pig's foot. Juniper found a pig in a nearby field, cut off its foot and cooked it.[10] The furious owner of the maimed pig came to complain to Francis, who berated Juniper for his lack of thought – and, interestingly, for endangering the brothers' reputation in the locality. After lengthy discussion and apology, the pig's owner eventually came to see that Juniper's motives were not malicious. The necessity to serve Christ by serving a sick man had blinded him to the consequences of his choice.

To the modern ear this story appears bizarre, even grotesque. The message it was intended to convey is easily masked by natural repugnance. Juniper's desire to live by the spirit of what he had been taught is difficult to fault. His obedience is to a higher authority than the law of ownership. Prompted by the gospel to care for the sick, he acts merely out of concern for his sick brother. Finally convinced by this argument, the pig's 'owner' comes eventually to question whether he has any more claim to the animal than Juniper does. The question of its suffering is not mentioned. In this analysis, Juniper's belief that he was serving Christ by responding to his brother's request is considered to outweigh the harm done.

The story of the pig is one of a number which celebrate Juniper's simple understanding of his faith and vocation. Depending on your point of view, Juniper can be an effective model of wholehearted simplicity. His desire to do only what God requires is laudably close to Francis' own. Too much thought, goes the argument, can inhibit the spontaneous response which alone communicates the free movement of the Spirit. There is a school of thought that Juniper was, in the old-fashioned sense, 'simple' – a person whose ability to take adult decisions and assess consequences was in some way impaired. This offers an interesting perspective. Like anyone else, the person with learning difficulties needs to be encouraged to take as much responsibility for decision-making as possible, in order to develop and grow. What is and is not appropriate can be explored *with* the person rather than imposed, even if only in very limited areas like what to eat or wear. There may always have to be someone in the background who is able to help point out the consequences of different courses of action; but they are being treated seriously, and thus assured of their value. Listening to somebody affirms the recognition that they have something valuable to say. It was when Juniper was able to explain himself both to Francis and to the outraged pig owner that a level of mutual understanding and acceptance was reached.

Alternatively, stories like this can give the impression that Franciscan spirituality condones irresponsibility in the name of childlike simplicity. If Juniper was not 'simple', *unable* to discern the effects of his choices, serious questions arise. The story of Juniper and the pig, meant to commend to its readers a model of Christlike simplicity of heart, unintentionally conveys a different message to contemporary readers. One mutilated pig is perhaps insignificant when reckoned against the human potential for cruelty to their own kind. However, everybody knows how the road to hell is paved. 'I was only obeying orders' is an all too familiar justification for some individual's unthinking part in any kind of atrocity. The same risk exists whether the orders in question are perceived as having come from God, from an institution such as the Church, or from some individual authority figure. For the adult afraid of the concomitant responsibilities of adulthood, being told what to do by somebody else can often appear the easier or more attractive option. Somebody else can then take the responsibility if things do go wrong. Power structures have their uses – and it is not always those who apparently hold the position of power who manipulate them most.

Unthinking obedience can be terribly damaging. It is also not particularly childlike: from a very early age children begin to ask 'Why?' In adolescence this becomes 'Why should I?' They need reasons to act. 'Because I say so', the standard response of the weary adult to repetitions of 'Why?', is unsatisfying because it is an exercise in power rather than a serious attempt at dialogue: if there is a response at all it will be compliance rather than listening obedience. The headmaster of a Benedictine public school in Britain, writing about the distinction between children, adults, and adults who behave like children, has said that what marks out childhood is the freedom from serious responsibility.[11] They are given responsibility commensurate to their age and level of maturity, but they need the safety of knowing that there are adults who will take over if they encounter a situation they can't handle. In order to enable children to develop a sense of responsibility at their own pace, they need that freedom, including the freedom to make mistakes.

Adult Children of God

There is a great difference between the childlike spontaneity of the 'simple' Juniper, acting impulsively out of pure zeal for the gospel, and the childish evasion of accountability by those too lazy to discern a proper response. For attentive obedience to work in any relationship, all parties have to be *capable* of taking adult responsibility for their own decisions. If they ultimately choose not to do so, they are not likely to live up to their full potential as human beings in the image of God.

Jesus taught us to call God 'Father'. The word he used, *Abba*, can be translated as Daddy. However, in using this name, Jesus was displaying the shocking intimacy which God seeks in his relationship with his people. It does not imply that God expects them to remain as literal children after it is time to grow further into his likeness. Children grow, and their relationship with their parents evolves as they do so. As their intimacy with God evolves and deepens, God's adult children are able to take more responsibility for their relationships with others. Growing beyond the need to shift blame, learning from past failure, those relationships have the potential for a mutuality from which a true, rich common life will be able to emerge.

The concept of the 'inner child' is a familiar one in the therapeutic world. Each person is, to a certain extent, shaped by the experiences, losses and joys of childhood. Patterns of relating learnt in infancy can become a framework, helpful or otherwise, for the future adult. Advances in self-knowledge and self-acceptance can be gained from allowing the 'inner child' to express feelings which perhaps went unheard earlier. From there, real growth, which might previously have been blocked by pain and regret, becomes a possibility. Childhood, however painful, is usually free of the weight of serious responsibilities. The adult who continues to cling fearfully to the patterns of childhood is a sad and stunted echo of the Father who wants all his children to reach their full potential.

Attentive to the cries of the suffering world, Christian listening must then be translated into action. Of course an adult sense of responsibility demands discernment as to the right *kind* of action. Not wanting to act precipitately, however, can become an excuse for not acting at all. Perhaps an 'adult' faith can too easily become cynical and disillusioned, tempered by harsh reality and an acceptance of 'the way things are'. The Franciscan life has to be open to the spontaneous prompting of the Spirit, whose message may disturb and disconcert, but must be heard. It is never an invitation to evade the realities of life. It is merely life lived in obedience to the Word spoken by God. All Christians share the responsibility to take that Word to heart in the way they live.

Genuine joy, a sense of fun and spontaneity which evokes the best of Franciscan living, need not be snuffed out by an ability to keep appropriate boundaries. Franciscan joy is found precisely in facing up to the cost of responding to life's pains and challenges as an adult child of God, sharing in the responsibility to bring about his Kingdom in service to his people.

Suggested Exercises

1. Set aside some time when you are sure of not being disturbed. Use your senses to become aware of your surroundings. Pay particular attention to what you can hear: birds, traffic, the hum of domestic machinery. (If you have impaired hearing, use another sense to relate to your physical surroundings.) Where is God for you, in the place and stage of life where you are now? Where might you begin to look for him?

2. Many people express difficulty with the idea of 'hearing' or 'listening to' God. Francis often 'heard' God's voice in the words of Scripture. Is there a verse or

passage which has particular significance for you, or which seems to recur at significant moments? What might it have to say to you now? If you are not familiar with Scripture, is there a poem or song which has the same effect?

Part Three
Joy

This joy, likewise, is a divine gift and comes only from union with God in Christ. As such it can abide even in days of darkness and difficulty, giving cheerful courage in the face of disappointment and an inward serenity and confidence in sickness and suffering. Those who possess it can be content with weaknesses, insults, hardships, persecutions, and calamities for the sake of Christ; for whenever they are weak, then they are strong.

(The Principles of the First Order of the Society of Saint Francis, Day 29)

7

Living with Difference

The brothers and sisters, rejoicing in the Lord always, must show forth in their lives the grace and beauty of divine joy. . . . They will carry with them an inner secret of happiness and peace which all will feel, if they may not know its source.

(*The Principles of the First Order of the Society of Saint Francis,* Day 28)

The Lasting Spirit of Francis

Why has the Franciscan life survived so long? What still prompts so many people to live out their Christian vocation in this particular way? The enthusiastic response down the centuries to Francis the person, and the way in which the legacy of his spirituality has evolved in new contexts and cultures, suggest that there is something timelessly attractive and compelling about his vision.

The joy and informality which characterize Franciscan life and worship at its best can be a breath of fresh air. Lives of Francis repeatedly tell of the joy which filled him as he spoke the name of the Lord, sang and danced in praise: 'wholly taken up in joy, filled with pure delight'.[1] But to be sustainable, such joyful outpourings must be nourished by deep and regular devotion to God.

Francis once described to Brother Leo his own unlikely vision of where perfect joy was to be found: not in miracles or religious ecstasy, nor in wisdom, but in hunger, cold, rejection and insult,[2] a life lived in imitation of the Christ who suffered and died. There remains a great need for the whole Church to take on board such a paradoxical vision of joy. Rejoicing with those who rejoice may seem easy, but the Church also needs to be seen as unafraid to weep with those who weep, showing them that God is to be found in the depths as well as the heights. Despite Francis' frequent insistence that his brothers should not look sad as they went about their work, in case they put people off, Franciscan joy is not to be equated simply with happiness. True joy may equally be found in listening to voices which can speak authentically of God's presence in the very midst of suffering. Finding God at work in the ordinary things of life, in rejoicing and in pain, the Franciscan way makes it possible to celebrate God's presence in the *whole range* of human experience.

Repent and Believe the Gospel

Celano says that anyone who intends to seek full perfection in the manner of Francis will need to 'put their hand to difficult things'. Many, he says, are afraid of such demands and prefer to settle for life on a lower level; but it is only in following Francis up the tricky slopes of complete immersion in God that perfect joy is to be found.

The unifying factor in all the themes of this chapter is penance. The concept of penance is an often overlooked aspect of Francis' theology. However, it is a very important one. The holy city of Jerusalem had been captured by Saladin's forces in 1187; the Fifth Crusade, called by Pope Innocent III after previous attempts had failed, was a rallying call to Christendom to try to win it back. The Crusades, as the name suggests, had at their centre the Cross. The figure of the Crucified, who had sacrificed his life for the sins of the world, was to be the inspiration for thousands to give up their own lives to redeem whatever wrong had led God to hand over Jerusalem to the infidels. Their failure to recapture it on any of the previous Crusades was surely a sign of his continuing displeasure. Constant prayers must be offered that God would once again come to favour their endeavours and reward Christian people with the return of 'their' holy city.

Francis was only five years old when Jerusalem fell to the Saracens. His whole vocation thus took shape in a context in which penance and sacrifice were widely discussed. Francis knew he had to reach awareness of the shortcomings of his early life before he could turn fully to God. The life of penance and self-denial he embraced was a deliberate sacrifice of self, in return for his new awareness of what Christ had sacrificed for him and for all people. Francis saw that it was nonetheless vital to a joyful, life-giving relationship with God and the world. In imitation of Christ, life was to be given up so it could be lived in abundance.

The urgency of Francis' call to repentance echoes John the Baptist. The message they shared was uncompromising: all people need to put themselves right with God, or else die, not just to this human life but to the chance of life everlasting. The *Canticle of the Creatures*, as well as celebrating Brother Sun and Sister Moon, contains the stark warning: 'Woe to those who die in mortal sin.' It is not a cosy concept, but neither can it be glossed over in any understanding of Francis' theology. Yet his preaching of penance was not based on emotional blackmail, or fear. The terms of the choice facing every human soul were made clear, but expressed with love: in the manner of Jesus telling the woman taken in adultery, 'Go, and do not sin again,'[3] Francis too pointed to a future of renewed hope.

Penance, for Francis, was a way of sharing in the pain of Christ at the imperfections of his world. It was during a long period of intense prayer on the passion of Christ that he received the marks of the stigmata. He never spoke of the wounds, even to his brothers, but kept them covered up. Carrying the wounds of Christ always with him in his flesh, Francis knew from the inside the pain of Christ – not just at the suffering of the world, but also at its failures, its refusal to be all it could be.

The language of penance may be thought to be unhelpful for many Christians, or ex-Christians, who find themselves crippled by a sense of guilt and wholly unable to accept the concept of a God of love. Yet in any relationship which has gone wrong, there is the need for confession and apology before healing can have any effect. While we are still busy justifying our behaviour and making excuses for it, we are not fully committed to putting right the relationship which has been damaged, whether it is with our next-door neighbour or with God.

Confession, whether sacramental or face-to-face with someone we have hurt, is an uncomfortable discipline because it is yet another reminder of our mutual dependence. Our actions and omissions do have consequences. We cannot live in complete isolation, either from other people or from the world. There is much to repent, too, in the way humans have distorted the relationship between ourselves, the most blessed of all the creatures, and the God who made us to be his stewards. Repentance demands a change of behaviour. If we are truly sorry for the way in which we have abused the earth and its creatures, we must be ready to embrace new ways of living in our environment. But repentance also offers a new start. Old wrongs and hurts can be put aside. There is always a second chance, a chance to come home.

Institution and Inspiration

'The obligation of particular obedience within the community is gladly accepted by the members, not as something different from the obedience which they owe to God, but rather as part of that obedience.'[4] In the spirit of the original Franciscan Rule, the *Principles* from which this quotation is taken also speak of obedience as an occasion of joy, finding perfection in the search for the divine wisdom.

Considering the Franciscan pattern of obedience to the will of God leads directly into an examination of Francis' relationship with the institutional Church and its structures. Christians have continually aspired to a pattern of behaviour modelled on Christ, and as continually fallen short. How do the structures within which Christians live out their faith themselves live up to the expectation that they should show Christ to the world? However necessary they are, structures and rules alone cannot save. Whether at the personal or institutional level, it is conversion to a more Christlike way of living that brings life.

Francis was suspicious of moves by some brothers to set up houses of learning. As we have seen, he knew his way round the Bible better than most, had some awareness of theology, and was familiar with the Latin of official church documents. He is reported as having a reverence for any piece of writing, however trivial, because the letters that made up any words were the same medium as those used to spell the name of God.[5] Yet scholarship was, by definition, the occupation of the rich and privileged. That was not what the order was for. The brothers were to serve God alone.

Francis' objection to over-intellectualizing the things of God is based in very practical reasoning. In a letter to Anthony of Padua he wrote: 'I am pleased that you teach sacred theology to the brothers providing that, as is contained in the Rule, you "do not extinguish the Spirit of prayer and devotion" during study of this kind.'[6] As so often, Francis' words prompt an important question. Is it necessary to be able to *understand* a way of life in order to proclaim it? Or is living it as much of a proclamation as we need? Joachim of Flora advocated conversion by word, not by sword; there could be no denying the power of the Word of God itself as a missionary tool. Francis' primary approach to preaching was by example and manner of life. *Thinking and writing* about God are not the same as experiencing God directly, and it was that direct experience which Francis knew to be paramount. God cannot be viewed objectively from a distance. God calls us into relationship, in which there is direct confrontation between our self and reality. Francis would not have used those words, but he would have known the experience. It cannot be adequately written about, but only sought, humbly, in prayer.

Anthony, Bonaventure and other brothers soon gave birth to a rich seam of Franciscan academic scholarship. It became clear that scholarship could be a genuinely valuable facet of Franciscan witness. But there is another reason why Francis may have been wary of encouraging too much concentration on it. In an age where to be able to read at all conveyed power, Francis was perhaps right to point out that the gift was to be handled with care. There is nothing wrong with learning *per se*. Indeed, it can be a powerful agent of liberation. It is those who use their learning to oppress others who should be challenged. The use and abuse of biblical scholarship down the ages proves this point only too clearly. The holy scriptures of most major religions have been manipulated in the same way to oppress or exclude. Sacred texts have been used to justify horrifying acts of violence and terrorism in every age. People and institutions of every faith have used them to sanction the appalling mistreatment of women, homosexuals, disabled people, Jews, slaves – the list, sadly, is endless.

The Church itself, as a repository of learning and the possessor of great truths, could be an immense liberating force. In some contexts it has been just that: the preaching of liberation to a people oppressed by secular forces has resulted in seismic change, for example in South Africa, where the theology of people like Desmond Tutu became a resource for the whole people of God. In other times and places, it is the Church itself which has used its knowledge to shore up its own power and become corrupted. Francis, who had such reverence for the Bible that he could not bear to see a copy left on the floor or covered up by any other book, did not just call individual sinners to repentance. He also sought to renew the whole body of the Church: where its power had enabled it to keep direct experience of God at a safe distance, it needed to be put back in touch with itself.

The Franciscan Rule

Mystic visionaries and eccentrics often don't fit neatly into existing structures – just as Jesus didn't! It is paradoxical that Francis, with his informal, spontaneous style, should be responsible for one of the major strands in religious life over the last eight centuries. He simply did what he saw it was necessary to do – to preach to a people who needed to hear the gospel – and people came to him. Such spontaneous response to God's will is, as we have seen, a keynote of the Franciscan way. Yet there *was* a need to regularize in order to survive as a force in the Church and the world, especially once Francis was no longer around. Francis himself arguably did not need a rule to tell him how to live; his essential rule book was the gospel. But as numbers grew, and structures had to be put in place for those living in other countries and areas where Francis himself could not be in frequent contact, there had to be guidelines to ensure the effective transmission of the founding vision. Furthermore, the official recognition of a rule by ecclesial authorities linked the new community more firmly with the body of the Church, affording it more protection in areas where small numbers or unfamiliarity might otherwise render it too vulnerable to be effective.

Both Francis and Clare made several attempts at producing a formal rule for their respective communities. In Clare's case, the struggle to have hers recognized and accepted by the Church took fifty years; she died within months of hearing that it had finally been given papal recognition. Women at that time had actually been debarred from forming any more religious orders, so Clare's insistence on following her vision and claiming the 'privilege' of poverty for herself and her sisters, as Francis did for his brothers, was a radical statement, underlining how strongly she felt that this was the right path for her.

Francis' original Rule was accepted by Innocent III in 1210, during a visit to Rome with the first eleven brothers. At this stage it was little more than a simple form of life, drawing heavily on the Gospels. It was considerably fleshed out in the Rule of 1221, which was agreed by the Chapter that year but was not promulgated, earning it the name of *Regula non bullata*: it is also known as the Earlier Rule. The text shows several influences from the fourth Lateran Council which had taken place a few years earlier, and from papal encyclicals of the same period.

The papal bull was finally received from Honorius III in November 1223. This final version of the Rule is a scant document of twelve short chapters. Compared to existing monastic rules such as St Benedict's, which sought to regulate every area of the monks' existence, it is remarkably unprescriptive. It is less detailed than the Earlier Rule of 1221, and arguably conforms more closely to existing ecclesial structures. On the Franciscan essentials, however, it is uncompromising: its heart and substance remain poverty, obedience, penance, preaching and prayer. These same elements characterize all attempts to live life as Francis did, in the pattern of Christ.

Francis and the Crusades

Over the last few years, there has been an increasing trend towards making official apologies for past wrongs. Governments, churches and other institutions which had been guilty of misusing their power in various ways began to make public acknowledgement of the false assumptions they had made in the past. Such acknowledgements, as well as prompting a rush of lawsuits, made it possible for old wounds to begin to heal.

It is only extremely recently that Christianity has ceased to assume that it is superior to other faiths. Growing up at the time of the Crusades, Francis shared the prevalent view that Christianity was the only truth. However, his obedience to God as a loyal Christian did not prevent him from treating adherents of other faiths with humanity. The encounter in 1219 between Francis and the Sultan in Damietta, on the coast north of Cairo, is a salutary example. Their meeting offers a potential model for present-day Christian–Muslim relations. Francis had tried to go once before, but bad weather made the journey impossible. In marked contrast to the usual beliefs and practices of his own day, Francis' approach to the Sultan indicates an unusual openness to difference. Neither was entirely persuaded by the other's arguments for his faith, but each recognized and valued sincerity in the other. The Sultan's hospitality and welcome earned Francis' respect, as Francis' refusal to be tempted away from poverty by exotic gifts impressed the Sultan. Francis' obedience to the promptings of God to share the gospel with all those around him thus led him to a surprisingly harmonious encounter with someone he might otherwise have been expected to fear or even hate.

Chapter 16 of the Rule of 1221, the so-called 'mission chapter', must have been influenced by Francis' encounters in the Muslim camp at Damietta. It gives very precise instructions to those brethren who feel called to visit the Holy Land. Its main argument is that mission is not just a matter of living among the Saracens, but also of being subject to them. Such an approach is all the more extraordinary in that Francis was here advocating something diametrically opposite to what his church was currently doing, and saying, in respect of Muslims. At best, they were considered as a form of heretic, believing in one God but denying the divinity of Christ. Their beliefs were often misrepresented in Crusade propaganda: the mistaken assertion that Muslims worship Mohammed as a divinity, rather than seeing him as God's prophet, was common. Being subject to them, in a world view which sought to impress Christian supremacy upon the infidels for the good of their immortal souls, was unthinkable. The mission chapter marks a shift in Francis' perspective. Brother Elias had been appointed Minister to the Holy Land in 1217, a few years before Francis' own journey. At that point, Elias' brief appears to have been more directly apologetic, preaching the gospel openly with the aim of winning souls for Christ. Likewise, in 1220, five friars were killed in Morocco, having been sent there to preach the gospel to the Moors. Francis' reaction on learning of their deaths was to commend them as the first 'true' friars, and they are recognized as the first Franciscan martyrs. This altered perspective, with less emphasis on outright missionary zeal and more recognition of common ground, thus emerged in his writing only after he had visited Morocco and the Holy Land for himself. Having heard how Muslims spoke of their faith, he was able to see that they too carried in them something of the image of God.

The knightly fame and fortune Francis had sought as a young man were on a local scale, in the wars between Assisi and Perugia. However, he could not have failed to be aware also of the wider scope for those intent on pursuing such a calling. As part of their contribution to the Crusade, all Christians were told to make their prayer for its success, to donate money for the upkeep of armies in the Holy Land, and to offer themselves for the fight, in the knowledge that they would be doing God's will. Any sacrifice of life in pursuit of this aim would be pleasing to him. Masses were to be offered for victory. Lay people too could be involved in God's sacrificial work; the Crusade was being presented as the spiritual quest of the whole Church. The willingness of ordinary Christians to volunteer for a task which might cost them their lives was held out to them as their way of imitation of Christ, as the priest imitates Christ at the altar. Francis, however, seems not to have been seduced by this rhetoric as he might once have been. For him the knightly path to glory was part of a past he had wholly rejected, a past of sin and shame. Glory, for him, was only to be attained by pursuing littleness.

Francis the Peacemaker

The call to do what he felt powerfully to be right sometimes led Francis to need to challenge the Church's leaders. Despite the respect and loyalty he felt for its priests, he was more concerned to speak what he felt to be the God-given truth than accept an orthodoxy which promoted violence over dialogue. The Dutch Franciscan scholar J. Hoeberichts points out in his book *Francis and Islam* that true dialogue between opposing points of view is impossible if one side enters the conversation convinced that it is superior. As with the leper or the wolf, Francis remained committed even in these emotive circumstances to listening to the actual voice of God, instead of the noise of prejudice.

Francis' generation saw the establishment of peace in Assisi as the commune took on responsibility for government from the nobility. However, this form of government by the people was seen as a potential threat to the power of the Church. Ecclesial authorities had therefore to reiterate that, even if mortals could control what happened to people's bodies, only the Church and its leaders could influence what happened to their immortal souls. Francis shared many of the same concerns. The ultimate goal for all Christians was eternal life. However, Francis' methods were different. He had no need to cling to power. He and his followers embraced the concept of *sine proprio*, without possessing or being possessed – without anything to possess, there is nothing to defend.

The most urgent contemporary application of Francis' legacy is his vocation as a peacemaker. Francis' readiness to be subject to others, even others who the institutional Church taught were inferior because they did not accept the Christian faith, is entirely consonant with his vision of himself and his brothers as always lesser. His desire to take Christ's pain and woundedness to himself stimulated him to live out Christian healing and wholeness in a damaged world.

Pope Innocent, in his letter declaring the Fifth Crusade and commending it to all the people of God, stresses that the Crusade could only hope to succeed if those who undertook it 'showed by their behaviour that they carried the wounds of Christ in their hearts'.[7] Francis would certainly have passed such a test. Yet he was able to do so without taking on board the Church's valuation of those who did not accept the faith it taught.

Francis could be said to have responded to the papal call to all Christians to become involved in the campaign, in that he did travel to the site where the Fifth Crusade was being fought. However, Celano's *Life* makes it clear that once there he still did not toe the papal line; instead, he felt it incumbent upon him on one occasion to tell the Christian forces that if they fought on a certain day they would lose.[8] This did not go down well; the 'forces of right' could not accept that God could possibly work against them. Francis' vision of God's will sometimes placed him at odds with the accepted structures. Unconditional support was the only proper response expected of a Christian for a battle ostensibly being fought in Christ's name. There are inevitable, and uncomfortable, echoes here of the righteous posturings of some of our present-day political leaders. Peacemaking does not make for popularity.

The Vision Evolves

Francis himself eventually recognized the need to step down from leading the order. He sometimes struggled with changes he himself would not have made. Elias, the brother who had visited the Holy Land as Minister in 1217, became Vicar of the order in 1221 and presided over the chapter which agreed the Earlier Rule. It was sometimes hard for Francis, and other brothers, to accept that changes in the structures of the community might actually enable future members to keep faith with its early inspiration. When someone takes over from a charismatic founder and leader, unfavourable comparisons will inevitably be made. Nevertheless, it is Elias and those who came after him who saw the need to renew the community's structures, so that Francis' original vision could live for future generations.

The ability to find joy in the strangest places is one sure hallmark of the unbroken Franciscan tradition. That same Franciscan joy, in being wherever Christ is, is now lived out in many forms and contexts throughout the world. The Franciscan family makes up the biggest single grouping of religious communities in the Christian churches. And Francis' joyful sincerity reaches beyond the boundaries of Christianity. Contemporary cynicism has not entirely snuffed out admiration for people who really believe wholeheartedly in the path they follow.

Sometimes God raises up figures like Francis who are able to speak directly to people's hearts and souls in any generation. All the contemporary expressions of Francis' vision are true in some respect to the original; but some have evolved in response to the unexpected demands of history or context. For example, Anglican Franciscans have existed for about a century. Additionally, there are now Franciscans in the Reformed churches in various parts of the world, as well as a continuing process of evolution of Franciscan life within the Roman Catholic Church.

The newly ecumenical dimension of Franciscan life has caused conflicts of loyalty for some. Francis' Rule explicitly stated his obedience to the Pope and his successors, commending his brothers to live in the same obedience.[9] Should all Franciscans then belong to the Roman Catholic Church, as Francis himself did? Can there be authentic expressions of the Franciscan life in churches which are not in communion with Rome? It is true that Francis took very seriously the sacraments and teachings of the church which nourished him. Although he was not beyond challenging the institution when he felt it necessary, there is no evidence to suggest that he ever envisaged anything else. Three hundred years before the Reformation, Francis could not have imagined the existence of other churches. It is often argued that the emergence of Franciscan life in churches beyond Rome reflects an obedience to the action of the Spirit in new contexts of which Francis could not have known, rather than slavish obedience to the letter of the Rule.

Francis' appeal, after all, is truly catholic, in the sense of universal. The Francis who engaged in conversation with the Sultan in Damietta would surely not condone an exclusive attitude towards any of God's creatures. Structures, however necessary, cannot be allowed to stifle the movement of the Spirit. Above all, Francis' reputation as a peacemaker and reconciler provides a powerful witness to what is possible when suspicion of difference is set aside in favour of listening. In a climate where ecumenism and interfaith dialogue have never been more important, Francis has much to teach us.

Suggested Exercises

1. Think of an episode in your life for which you feel you still need to repent. Don't allow yourself to spend too much time on what you might have done or said differently, but be as honest as you can about what actually happened. You may find it helpful to share your feelings with another person, perhaps a priest or minister, or to write them down. How does it feel to

bring this situation to God? Is there anything practical you can realistically do to rectify it?

2. What brings you real joy? What might you still need to do, or to let go, in order to find it?

8

Mirror of Perfection

Place your mind before the mirror of eternity!
Place your soul in the brilliance of glory!
Place your heart in the figure of the divine substance!
And transform your whole being into the image of the
  Godhead Itself through contemplation
so that you too may feel what His friends feel
as they taste the hidden sweetness
which God Himself has reserved from the beginning
for those who love Him.

(St Clare, *Third Letter to Blessed Agnes of Prague*)[1]

It has already been argued that Francis' own compulsion
to lead a life of poverty and simplicity can be traced to
his origins in the mercantile class. His companion St
Clare made an identical option for poverty. In her case it
can be linked to the expectations of an aristocratic
family in thirteenth-century Italy.

Chiara Offreduccio di Favarone was born some eleven
or twelve years after Francis. She has been referred to as
the feminine principle in the Franciscan movement,[2] the
first woman to be directly inspired to live in his way.
However, she is not merely 'Francis in a veil', or Francis
enclosed: the feminine expression she and her sisters gave
to the Franciscan charism is authentic, but distinctive.

Like Francis, Clare left little in the way of her own
writing. Until relatively recently, her place in the Franciscan story has been largely obscured. However, her
influence on the development of Franciscan spirituality
cannot be overestimated. Perhaps because of the essentially hidden, enclosed nature of her life at San Damiano,
perhaps because she was a woman, perhaps because she
does not seem to have undergone the same dramatic conversion experiences that Francis did, she has never quite
achieved the same prominence as Francis himself. The
rebirth of interest in Franciscan spirituality around the
turn of the twentieth century brought many people to
consider some kind of active service among the poor.
However, the contemplative ingredient of Francis' own
vocation has often been overlooked. A study of Clare,
and the interweaving of her vocation with that of
Francis, can help to redress that balance.

The *Legend of St Clare*, written soon after her death
at the request of the then Pope, Alexander IV, says that
Clare's father was a knight,[3] the status to which the
youthful Francis had himself aspired. Her mother,
Ortolana, is described as a devout and holy woman.
From the description of Ortolana's life of 'divine worship, the works of piety [and] devout pilgrimage',[4] it is
possible that she belonged to the movement which has
come to be known as the Beguines. These were a group
of lay women, often married with a family, who would
meet together for mutual support in the life of prayer,
and would sometimes undertake pilgrimages together;
Ortolana is said to have journeyed with others to several
places sacred to the Christian faith, among them the

Holy Land. These devout women thus combined a loose form of religious life with marriage, motherhood and other obligations. The *Legend* depicts the infant Clare laying out the rosary in pebbles in the garden, a nice example of how children tend to imitate the preoccupations of their parents.

Unlike Francis, Clare seems to have felt the call to poverty and religious life very young. For her there was to be no dramatic conversion, rather a confirmation of what she seems always to have known: that the world, and the material benefits of her upbringing, were not for her. She is therefore part of a hagiographical tradition which honoured purity and virginity, the supreme example being Christ's own mother. According to the *Legend*, as a small child Clare secretly gave away what she could to the poor, under the 'impulse of holy love'. As her generosity became known, she began to acquire a local reputation for piety and purity. Even before her path first crossed with Francis', the accounts of Clare's early life thus give the impression of steady, unwavering progress towards a goal which never shifted.

The Making of a Saint

At the period in which Francis and Clare lived, the publication of a definitive Life was a required part of the canonization process for any saint. The *Legend of St Clare*, like the official Process of Canonization, offers a description of Clare's life based on the testimony of various people who knew her. Like Francis, Clare was recognized as a saint within her own lifetime and the canonization process began almost immediately after her death in 1253: the *Legend* was written and circulated within about eighteen months of that date. Its authorship is uncertain, though many scholars believe that it was the work of Thomas of Celano, who had also been responsible for two prose Lives of St Francis as well as a liturgical version for use in services. His Lives of Francis certainly stress the strong links between the two saints.

Hagiographies liked to make much of dramatic conversion stories. The more debauched the subject's early life had been, the more compelling was their later choice of holiness. The audience was intended to grasp that such a choice was therefore possible for anyone: no matter what wrong turnings a life had previously taken, Christ could transform it. The first few chapters of Francis' own life as described by Celano emphasize that very process, highlighting the change in him and thus making his later achievements in the name of Christ seem all the more remarkable. Clare, by contrast, represents a different strand of writing about saints. Some of those who read or heard such accounts of conversion in the lives of the saints would be encouraged to try to break away from their own sinful ways. Those who had always lived reasonably virtuous lives, however, would have no need of drastic alteration in lifestyle. Instead, they needed encouragement to believe that God would reward their perseverance in the way of faith. The *Legend of St. Clare* paints a picture of such lifelong, determined Christian discipleship, from which no hardship could deflect her.

Much has been made of the symbolic way in which

Clare left her family's house to come to Francis. On the night when she ran away to join the brothers at the Little Portion, she apparently broke open the 'dead gate', normally used for removing corpses from the house and otherwise kept sealed, and left that way rather than by the main door. Her choice resonates with the themes of death to self which underpinned Francis' own vocation; in choosing to leave in the way she did, Clare was pronouncing a sentence of death on her old life and her family's hopes for an advantageous marriage. It has been suggested by some Clare scholars that part of the scandal, from her family's point of view, was that during her brief period in the Benedictine convent of San Paolo at Bastia, she was used by the community there as a lay sister. These were usually uneducated women who acted as servants to the rest of the community. Girls of Clare's aristocratic background would normally have joined as choir nuns, whose work was prayer and scholarship. Hildegarde of Bingen, born in Germany a century or so before Clare, was educated by nuns from a very young age and, as Abbess at Bingen, became a notable preacher, musician, herbalist and confidante of bishops. As the daughter of a knight, Clare too would have been educated to a higher standard even than the allegedly 'unlettered' Francis. To be a lay sister would have been considered a social disgrace for such a woman. Poverty itself was an unthinkable choice; small token 'mortifications of the flesh' were one thing, but a life of 'actual penury and extreme simplicity'[5] was quite another. However, this was the path on which Clare was set. Like Francis her inspiration, she too was in love with poverty, and nothing could be allowed to distract her from that purpose.

When members of her family did track her down and come to take her back, Clare clung to the altar, and could not be detached from it. A similar story is told about her sister Catherine, who later joined her in religious life at San Damiano and was given the name Agnes. Again, the men of the family came to try to take her away, but Agnes miraculously grew so heavy that they could not move her, and they had to leave her there. Like Clare, she persevered in her vision; many years later, she provided one of the testimonies in the canonization documents for her sister.

Clear Shining Light

When Ortolana was nearing the end of her pregnancy with Clare, the *Legend* states that she went to pray before the crucifix for a safe delivery. In a strange parallel with Francis' experience in San Damiano, as yet several years in the future, Ortolana heard a voice as she prayed. It told her that the child in her womb would be 'a light to illumine the world'. As so often in Francis' own story, here too there is a clear echo of the life of Christ, this time of the infancy narrative in the Gospel of Luke. There is a marked similarity between the wording of Ortolana's vision and those used by the old man Simeon to Mary and Joseph as they present the baby Jesus in the temple; in the prayer now commonly known from its Latin translation as the Nunc Dimittis, he praises God for allowing him to see the Messiah in the form of this child, and tells the baby's parents that their son will be 'a light for revelation to the Gentiles'.[6] Ortolana's response to her own revelation was to insist that her baby be baptized Chiara, which means 'clear' or 'light'. Medieval literature often draws parallels between outward appearance and the state of the soul. Like the romance heroines of the period, Clare's physical beauty and fair colouring were seen as evidence of her spiritual perfection. Her presence was seen as giving light to a church grown dark with corruption and power.

According to the conventions of medieval hagiography, circulated versions of saints' lives would stress – perhaps even exaggerate – any similarities with Christ's own life. As with the conversion stories, this was done in order to provoke listeners to greater piety, and to encourage them to emulate their example. Even so, the lives of Francis and Clare provide some striking parallels. For example, Francis' mother, Pica, was supposed to have given birth to him in a stable behind the family house. As is still the case today, some documented evidence of miracles was required before a case could be made for canonization. The Lives duly recount several stories in which both Francis and Clare heal a number of people from various physical and mental afflictions. Other miracles are documented, both during and after their earthly lives: multiplication of loaves and other food, nature miracles, even raising people from the dead, all of which echo the events of Christ's own ministry. Whatever the literal truth behind such incidents, the implication is that both Francis and Clare were in some way marked out from the beginning of their lives to live as closely as possible in imitation of their Lord. It also shows that they did try to live as Christ lived – whether or not the events described are literally true, their inclusion does highlight the efforts of both Francis and Clare to *become* more like their Master.

Clare and Francis

From Clare's first encounter with Francis when she was about sixteen or seventeen, she was immediately captivated by his enthusiasm, his preaching, and the way in which he appeared 'afire with God'. As described in Chapter 4, Clare's family were keen that she should marry someone who could enhance their standing, and Francis' background in the merchant class meant that he would not have fitted the profile of a suitable husband for a girl of knightly birth, even if he had wanted to. The *Legend* says that they used to meet secretly, for fear of causing gossip locally. Some fictionalized versions of their respective Lives have speculated about the exact nature of the relationship between Francis and Clare. However, the tone of Clare's writings on virginity, and the singlehearted zeal for God which she shared with Francis, make it unlikely that there was ever a romantic attachment in the sense in which we might understand it today. Yet there was undeniably a strong emotional and spiritual bond. In her own writing, Clare referred to herself as a 'little plant' of St Francis,[7] and to Francis as the planter, to whom she saw herself and her sisters as obedient. For his part, Francis wrote of his 'loving care and special solicitude' for Clare and her Poor Ladies.[8] Both of them specifically commended a continuing relationship to their respective communities in their writing.

In a dream or vision, recounted by a number of separate witnesses in the Process of Canonization, Clare once saw herself as a nursing child suckling at Francis' breast and nourished by the sweet milk she found there. It would, however, be a mistake to see the nourishment and inspiration as going only one way. Francis himself spoke of Clare with great affection and respect. Their vocations ran in parallel, expressing different aspects of a common call in which they were each other's greatest support and inspiration. Clare's pattern of continued enclosure offered a safe place for Francis to go when he needed advice, and sometimes solace, yet still to be surrounded and steeped in prayer. The *Canticle of the Creatures*, according to another early source known as the *Legend of Perugia*, was written at San Damiano during a period of illness towards the end of his life. Clare is now credited by many theologians with having kept the Franciscan vision alive during the years after Francis' death when it could easily have died out or become corrupted.

The Order of Saint Clare is also known as the Second Order, as it was the second of the three orders, each with their own distinctive vocation, which were directly inspired by Francis. Clare shared Francis' deep love of the poor Christ and of literal poverty. Her insistence on the 'privilege of poverty' led to her community becoming known in her lifetime as the Poor Ladies, and later as the Poor Clares. Although this unusual right not to have possessions or endowments was granted to the Poor

Ladies as early as 1216, Clare still had a long struggle ahead of her before she was truly able to live the life to which she felt called. Rules had been written for the community by Cardinal Hugolino and Pope Innocent IV, but both were fundamentally Benedictine in form and vision. Neither fully expressed her commitment to a specifically Franciscan way of life. The papal bull accompanying the final form of the Rule in 1253 at last acknowledges her overwhelming desire to live in poverty for the sake of 'freedom of soul'.[9]

Clare had a significant effect on the development of Francis' thought, preaching and prayer life. Her own spirituality is distinct, but intimately interwoven with his. She is an example of how people down the ages have been able to take the essence of Francis and do something very different with it. Commentators differ as to whether she might, in another age, have wanted to emulate Francis in an active lifestyle not then possible for women religious. From her writings, however, it seems likely that for her the contemplative life was not a restriction; rather, the pursuit of contemplative prayer in the context of enclosed community life was her distinctive gift to the Franciscan tradition.

The Mirror of Eternity

The imagery of light crops up again and again in the *Legend* and other writings on Clare: words like 'brilliant' and 'radiant' occur frequently. The *Legend* describes the urgent need for spiritual renewal in the Church, which had grown dark with sin and corruption before Clare's holy example came to enlighten it. She in turn refers to Christ as illuminating and the Holy Spirit as enlightening.

The image of the mirror and of reflection has already cropped up several times in preceding chapters. It is central to Clare's theology. She did not leave much written record of her thought, but in her letters to Agnes of Prague (another young woman of noble birth determined to live in loving simplicity), as well as in her Rule and *Testament*, the imagery of the mirror is absolutely fundamental. Christ is the mirror of all human beings, in which we can see ourselves reflected with more or less distortion. The role of all Christian people is also to reflect that image of Christ on into the world. Clare's sisters were to provide that same reflection for each other, in the way they lived community together. Their life was also intended as an example and inspiration for those who lived outside. Mirrors show a reverse image of what really is: in the mirror of contemplative community, the values of the world are turned back to front. God is no longer pushed to the edge, but is found at the very centre. Clare's perception of Christ as mirror allows him to take his true place at the heart of life.

The medieval mirror was more likely to be made of beaten metal than of glass. The accuracy of its reflection was therefore dependent on how finely polished the surface was, or how many distorting bumps it had. Preparing the surface would thus enable it to show a truer likeness. When Clare tells Agnes of Prague to gaze daily on her face in the mirror of Christ, she is instructing her to prepare herself more and more completely to see Christ looking back at her from the depth of the mirror. Jesus himself, hanging on the cross, is a mirror of what Christians are called to become. The frame of the mirror is his poverty, the context in which we are able to see him and relate to him. The reality of his becoming human is that he shares our life in all its unevenness, even before the lumps have been smoothed out. Looking into the surface of the mirror, where work has been done to prepare and burnish the soul in order to provide a better reflection, we can gain understanding of the way Christ lived, and seek to emulate it. But it is only in the very depth of the mirror, at the point where the gaze meets infinity, that the soul can merge completely with Christ.

Other important themes in Clare's theology include the Eucharist. She shared Francis' devotion to the passion of Christ, and his desire to be part of it through the sacrament. Clare was credited with repelling a Saracen invasion of her monastery by holding out a silver pyx containing the Body of Christ, whose purity they were unable to withstand.[10] Her devotion to the mass and the Blessed Sacrament were spoken of by many witnesses in the Process of Canonization, which fleshes out the biographical detail of the Legend. Clare's eucharistic devotion can also be seen as an extension of her image of Christ as mirror – in this act of sacrifice, we see Christ as he truly is, without distortion. At the moment of communion, the soul reaches the point of encounter with God at the heart of the mirror, where image and reality merge.

Being and Doing

Francis and Clare are complementary mirrors of each other's experience. Clare was motivated as Francis was by the life of the gospel, yet content that her particular observance of that life took her in another direction. Where Francis writes about his brothers as a group of individuals with varied expressions of a common purpose, Clare consistently uses the language of community and common mind. She may thus have even more challenging things to say to the contemporary obsession with individualism.

A reading of her Rule shows that great emphasis was placed on what we might now call the quality of community life, and her relationships with her sisters were said to be characterized with great kindness and generosity. Her model of leadership, like Francis', is diaconal: washing her sisters' feet, serving them in the refectory, caring for them in sickness. There is honest recognition of how individual sisters' needs may vary,[11] and a loving desire to meet such needs without detracting from the purpose of community life. Those living the common life are further encouraged to mutual accountability by weekly meetings where problems may be addressed. Such provision was essential for the maintenance of healthy relationships in an enclosed environment. She was also flexible in the interpretation of that enclosure and the existence of life beyond the walls. There is no hint here of contemplative withdrawal prompted by disgust of the world. Like Francis, Clare finds in all human beings her brothers and sisters. It is merely that for her, freedom to relate is greater within four walls. Enclosure is seen by those who truly live it not as a negative, a repudiation of the world, but as a place where God can be encountered without distraction, a power-house of love.

There was always a discernible tension in Francis' own life between profound personal engagement with human need and periods of solitary contemplation on La Verna. Held in balance with necessary activity, times of aloneness with the Alone fuel community life both at the individual and the corporate level. Francis and Clare's shared vocation to contemplation, whether enclosed or not, echoes the world's need for more *prayer*. The life of prayer is the place where contemplation becomes action, where God's purpose and human desire are brought together. Everyone lives with limited spiritual resources, in a world which needs constant reminders of where its attention should be. Christians believe that prayer can make a difference. It is not just a cheap spiritual feelgood fix. Nor is it about scratching the back of a despotic God who needs to be worshipped.

However feeble and inadequate an intervention it may be, in an otherwise intractable situation prayer is an attempt to 'do something': by focusing on the reality of God's presence in that situation, new avenues of hope and possible action may be opened up. Simone Weil pointed out that prayer consists of attention. Strictly speaking, there is no need to bring a particular situation to God's attention. Rather, prayer is about bringing God to the world's attention. In his suffering or questioning people, God is already present and active before anyone invokes him. The purpose of prayer is to let God be God, and to make his activity visible to those who need to see it.

As Francis and his brothers found, there will always be a certain tension in the Christian life between the need to '*do something*' and be seen to be of use, and the need to take time to be alone with God. The early history of the First Order shows how the brothers came to struggle with the contradictory parts of Francis' original vision for it, a struggle which is still not fully resolved. There is constant debate as to the value and importance of each in the Christian life in general. In community life, where there is often too much needing to be done and not enough people to do it, this can sometimes take a pointed form. 'Being' can become a jealously guarded luxury rather than a vital breathing space for the soul. Yet both of these two strands are equally necessary to the balanced spiritual life. Franciscan spirituality stands at the meeting of the two.

In a world where so many are in need of practical help, a life devoted to prayer can seem unjustifiably self-indulgent. Clare's contribution to the developing story of the Franciscan family has been to show enclosed contemplation as something positive in itself; not as second best for those unable to engage actively with the world, but as a driving force behind a change in focus. The breadth of Franciscan spirituality is a challenge and irritant to today's priorities. In a world of conflicting noises, the call to silent contemplation can be heard as an invitation to *pay attention*, to return to reality at the heart of the mirror.

The Catholic writer Catherine de Hueck Doherty

commented that 'it is the poor who pray': in other words, those who are most aware of their insufficiency and dependence, who cannot buy their way into comfortable oblivion. Clare and her sisters, with nothing to hold them or distract them, are witnesses to the value of life lived on such terms. Constant attentiveness to God means living always at the heart of the mirror, seeing all things with the loving clarity of God himself.

Suggested Exercises

1. How do you pray best? If you can set aside a regular time for prayer, try spending it in a way which is less familiar – maybe using movement, or painting, or music, or silence and stillness, or words for God other than those you would habitually use. It doesn't matter how good or bad you feel you are at any of these things; just notice how it makes you feel to do them. What do you learn about God? And about yourself?

2. Examine your face in a mirror. What do you especially like or dislike about your appearance? Can you see yourself as made in the image of God? What holds you back from being able to see yourself in that way?

9

Faith in the Real World

*I have done what was mine to do; may Christ show you
what is yours to do.*

(St Francis of Assisi)[1]

Prayer and Life

Franciscan spirituality continues to draw people from
the most unlikely situations. Perhaps the fastest growing
area of Franciscan vocation today is in the Third Order,
or Secular Franciscan Order as it is called in the Roman
Catholic Church. Like the brothers and sisters of the first
two Orders, this distinctive pattern of Franciscan discipleship was directly inspired by Francis, as people
sought to honour their own Christian vocation without
compromising existing commitments to family or work.
Pursuing a deeper Christian discipleship for themselves,
as Francis had to point out to some of them, should
never be allowed to become an excuse for escaping from
costly personal obligations. Faith can only ever be lived
out in the real world, working within the web of commitment and relationship surrounding each human
being. To this end, he encouraged those who were eager
for such a commitment to draw up a simpler version of
the Rule followed by the brothers and sisters; this Rule

took into account their different circumstances and offered realistic spiritual goals with the support of like-minded people. It continues to draw people with an enthusiasm for Francis and the pattern of spirituality which bears his name. Even those who do not want to make a formal commitment to join the Franciscan family can find lasting inspiration in the life and prayer of the rich man's son who challenged so deeply the values of his world and his church. No institution can afford to ignore the questions he posed. Like his master Jesus Christ, Francis' challenge was issued without violence and without arrogance. There is no attempt to bully or shame people into living in a way which compromises their integrity. The good news of gospel living is merely presented in a way which makes it possible to choose freely.

We have explored many factors about the original Franciscan vision which might explain why it continues to compel so many people to follow that particular Christian path. Much writing on religious life in previous generations has been adversely affected by a belief that the way it describes is in some sense a higher calling than 'life in the world', rather than being one of a range of complementary vocations. A dangerous duality was thus perpetuated between what were perceived to be the things of the world, and the things which properly belonged to God. Both Francis and Clare have offered a corrective to this approach over eight centuries. Their faith is absolutely rooted in the real, day-to-day engagement of one human being with another, and of all creatures with their God. Commitment in the Franciscan mould celebrates the world as God created it. Religious life takes its place in the pattern of Christian discipleship as one of a number of ways in which each created being is called uniquely to use his or her gifts and weaknesses in the service of God.

Theirs, too, is a view of community living which challenges any inappropriate idealism about the religious life or the sort of people who pursue it. Instant holiness is not an option. The poverty common to every human person is all too apparent in every kind of Christian community. The struggle to live Christian discipleship in any form is littered with failed attempts to encounter others as they are. Poverty of love, of patience and of welcome cannot be overcome simply by taking vows. Yet the vows which sustained Francis and Clare have something of value for every Christian. Then as now, their love of poverty provided a stark contrast with the prevailing ideology that humanity's prior purpose is to succeed, preferably by amassing material wealth and status. Poverty, says the Anglican Benedictine theologian Harry Williams, 'takes pleasure in a thing because it is'.[2] Chastity, too, is impossible without a refusal to possess. It is not to be achieved simply by abstention from certain bodily activities, but must be characterized by a loving singleheartedness in every relationship. Franciscan obedience is the open, risky surrender of the whole personality to God. It is rooted in that sense of relatedness which, as we have seen, makes it impossible to say 'this person is not my concern' without becoming dangerously detached from the message of the gospel. All three vows thus speak powerfully to our contemporary dilemma as people of faith in a world awash with confusion.

Franciscan living is characterized by transparency. In humility, love and joy, Francis and Clare lived in constant awareness of the presence of God – in themselves, in each other, and in their brothers and sisters throughout the whole of creation. Willing to become fools for Christ's sake, their simplicity challenged the accumulated wisdom of their own age. Their way of life was marked by joy without irresponsibility, humility without false modesty, and a Christlike love without restraint. With authenticity and integrity as the benchmark of each relationship, they were able to be always open, to hear the voice of God equally clearly in the mundane and the surprising. The spirituality of Francis and Clare shows how the ordinary is transformed when we learn to see with the eyes of God. The essential characteristics of Franciscan spirituality are therefore not divorced from the joys and difficulties of everyday living, but remain intimately connected with them. If we dare seek to live in such a way ourselves, we may come to resemble more closely not only Francis and Clare, but the Lord and Saviour who never ceased to attract and call them.

Franciscan Relevance for Today

Attempts to describe contemporary Western culture frequently throw up words like fragmented, isolationist, individualistic, self-determining and self-realizing. There is a tendency to represent 'community' as something desirable as a corrective to this perceived fragmentation – but less willingness, perhaps, to acknowledge the

necessary process of mutual listening and accountability
involved in realizing it. Community, if it is not to become
stifling or self-indulgent, has constantly to be worked at
by those who live it. It is not merely the responsibility of
the leaders, but of each member, to become vulnerable
enough to be known so that they too may know others as
their brothers and sisters. Such intimacy is at once enti-
cing and threatening. The recent fascination with 'reality'
television programmes like *Big Brother*, in which arbi-
trarily selected groups of people are made to live
together and every detail of their interaction is filmed,
stems from an absorption with community, and a need
to discover the communities to which each of us belong,
in order to understand ourselves as we are. The attraction of institutions may have faded, along with automatic trust in what they provide; but the urge to belong,
and to define ourselves by our patterns of belonging, has
not.

'Who is my neighbour?' remains an essential question.
The Franciscan vocation to peacemaking challenges the
territorial mindset that clings to the need to destroy anyone who threatens our sense of self or of security. If we
are not to be deafened to the voice of the other by our
constant anxiety at the possibility of global destruction,
we need Franciscan courage. This is the courage to
become lesser: to take the risk of loving without possession, and face the reality of being loved or rejected in
return. The central Franciscan concept of littleness has a
powerful value and usefulness today. It reminds us that
being lesser need not be in collision with our need to
have a balanced view of our worth and our rights; but it

should, perhaps must, be in collision with the assertion of materialist culture that I should be able to grab whatever I want when I want it and never mind at whose expense. 'If they will but be emptied of self and utterly surrendered to him, they will become chosen vessels of his Spirit and effective instruments of his mighty working.'[3] To be little is to have less to cling to, less that may get in the way of us doing what *God* wants.

Safe in our own carefully constructed environment, we long for a sense of *relatedness*, of significance to someone or something beyond ourselves. The quiet presence of Franciscans (and others) in the 'untouchable places' of the world can be a sign of God's continued presence to, and existence in, the pain of the world as well as in its obvious successes. God's standards are not ours.

Franciscan down-to-earthness has everything to do with a desire to embrace life as it really is, and as God intended it to be. As we saw at the beginning of Chapter 1, 'Humility is the recognition of the truth about God and ourselves'. The humble realism of Francis and Clare involves seeing and loving the world as it is. So must God have looked on his creation, and seen that it was very good. This realism extends to all creatures, but it is perhaps most striking when lived out to the full among our own kind, in all our sinfulness and limitation. But a Franciscan vision cannot stop there. In our very littleness and insignificance there is nevertheless a limitless potential to reflect God. In the right deployment of power and greatness, too, God's generosity can be mirrored. Everything, seen and loved for what it truly is, can be brought into harmony, to work together in a song of praise and thanksgiving to the Creator of all.

Francis and Clare teach us to see without cynicism, without pretence or pretension. The great Franciscan theologian, Bonaventure, demonstrated this when the Church declared him a cardinal. Several times he failed to respond to the invitation, until at last they came to find him, bringing with them the cardinal's hat so that he should not refuse it. When the deputation arrived, they found him doing household tasks; unimpressed, he merely hung the hat on a tree until his work was complete.

How does this emptying of self marry with the insistence, both contemporary and absolutely true to God's vision for his people, that we fulfil ourselves? Again, we find here not contradiction but unexpected fruition. As with so much of the Franciscan message, the truth is to be found in the opposite of the usual values of the world. The Franciscan vocation echoes the vocation of all Christians – and indeed of each of the great religions – for *all* people to be enabled to be fully human. Inhabiting the world together with those we acknowledge as our brothers and sisters, even those we do not know or do not like, we can learn to facilitate and celebrate the fullness of others around us.

Francis and Clare were not trivial people, despite their lightness of touch and evident sense of fun. They were both childlike in their simplicity and singleness of purpose, but in no way immature. Their demands on themselves, and on those who followed them, were intense. Yet their story also makes clear that the rewards were great. A life lived as they lived, with absolute integrity of purpose, without evasion or falsehood, aggression or posturing, is the greatest possible imitation of Christ. The only response adequate to God's amazing generosity to us is to allow ourselves to undergo radical transformation into the people God wants us to be.

There have been many attempts over the years to retell aspects of the story of Francis and Clare, and to apply what they taught to successive generations. In fictional as well in scholarly versions, something of the persuasive original vision is communicated to a modern understanding, as the early legends and lives did for the people of their own time. Yet people are often unwilling to let Francis and Clare speak, as they want to speak, of the limitless love and beauty of God. We are usually too comfortable as we are to allow ourselves to open our minds and hearts in listening obedience. Our comfort zones make us unwilling to put Christ at the centre as they ask us to; unwilling to embrace today's lepers, unwilling to give up our security in order to follow the risky path to perfect joy. Francis' description of that perfect joy, in rejection and physical hardship, is far from alluring! The cost of complete simplicity has proved too high for most of us. But true Franciscan living is always recognizable by its unexpected fruits. Despite the contradictions and difficulties inherent in following the Gospel wholeheartedly in any age, the Franciscan way of humility, love and joy will bring to those who risk it 'an inner secret of happiness and peace, which all will feel, if they may not know its source'.[4]

Suggested Exercise

You might like to consider drawing up a simple rule of life for yourself. Such a rule need not be a burden or a straitjacket for your relationship with God, but a framework within which you can grow. Some things to include might be:

- A *realistic* time of prayer each day, depending on your existing commitments and your energy level. You can always build it up gradually!

- Making space for other ways to spend time with God, e.g., making a commitment to attend church, Bible reading, retreats.

- Finding constructive ways to work on relationships – with family, friends, colleagues, God and yourself.

- Giving to charity, voluntary work, or some other commitment to put your faith into action (eg writing letters for Amnesty International).

Notes

(Place of publication London unless otherwise stated)

Introduction

1. Archbishop Rowan Williams, *Writing in the Dust*, Hodder & Stoughton, 2002, chapter 1.
2. Matthew 19:21.
3. T.S.Eliot, 'Little Gidding', in *Four Quartets*, Faber and Faber, 1963.

Part One: Humility

1 Life and Context

1. St Clare of Assisi, *Testament*, in Regis J. Armstrong and Ignatius C. Brady, eds, *Francis and Clare: The Complete Works*, Mahwah, NJ, Paulist Press, 1982, p. 226.
2. Geoffrey Willans and Ronald Searle, *The Compleet Molesworth*, Pavilion Books, 1985.
3. Galatians 2:20.
4. Thomas of Celano, *Life of Saint Francis*, First Book, chapter I. (Referred to hereafter as 1 Cel. Celano's second Life of Saint Francis, also known as *The Remembrance of the Desire of a Soul*, is referred to as 2 Cel.)
5. 1 Cel. II.
6. *A Mirror of the Perfection*, 32, in Regis J. Armstrong, J. A. Wayne Hellmann and William J. Short, eds, *Francis of Assisi: Early Documents*, New York, New City Press, 1999–2001 (referred to hereafter as FED 1–3), vol. 3, p. 242.

7. Matthew 23:9.
8. Matthew 19:21.

2 *God with Us*

1. *The English Hymnal.* By permission of Novello & Co. Ltd.
2. *The Alternative Service Book 1980.*
3. See Philippians 2:6–11.
4. Psalm 139.
5. *The Principles of the First Order of the Society of Saint Francis,* revised 1996, Day 13. (Referred to hereafter as *The Principles.* Divided into sections for daily reading and reflection over the course of a month.).
6. *The Principles,* Day 30.
7. Brother Angelo SSF, 'Francis and Brother Ass', *Franciscan,* January 1996.
8. Brother Angelo SSF, 'Francis and Brother Ass'.
9. Rowan Clare CSF, 1995. ©The European Province of the Community of Saint Francis.

3 *Gospel Living*

1. Prayer of St Francis before the Crucifix, FED 1, p. 40.
2. The *Testament of St. Francis,* 14, FED 1, p. 125.
3. The *Later Rule* (1223), chapter I, FED 1, p. 100.
4. The *Testament of St. Francis,* 5, FED 1, p. 124.
5. Archbishop Rowan Williams, unpublished address to Millennium Conference of Anglican Religious Communities, Swanwick, September 2000.
6. Matthew 19:21.
7. Luke 2:49.
8. 1 Corinthians 1:25.
9. Job 2:13.
10. Sister Rose CSF, 'One of the least . . .', in *Franciscan,* May 1997.
11. Sister Rose CSF, 'One of the least . . .'.

12. St. Francis of Assisi, *Admonitions* XXVII, FED 1, pp. 136–7.
13. Meister Eckhart, 'On the noble man', *Liber Benedictus*, part 2, in *Selected Writings*, trans. Oliver Davies, Penguin, 1994.

Part Two: Love

1. John 13:35.

4 Poverty

1. The *Earlier Rule*, chapter VIII, FED 1, p. 69.
2. Frances Teresa OSC, *Living the Incarnation*, DLT, 1993, p. 14.
3. 1 Cel. XIX.
4. The *Earlier Rule*, chapter VI, FED 1, p. 68.
5. 2 Corinthians 6:10.
6. Prologue to *The Sacred Exchange Between St. Francis and Lady Poverty*, FED 1, p. 529.
7. 1 Cel. XV.
8. Mark 14:36.
9. Exodus 3:14.

5 Song of Creation

1. St Francis of Assisi, *Canticle of the Creatures*, FED 1, p. 113.
2. Psalm 8, in *The Daily Office SSF*, Mowbray, 1992.
3. 1 Cel. XXIX.
4. 1 Cel. XXIX.
5. 2 Cel. LXXVII.
6. Mark 11:13–14.
7. 1 Cel. XXI.
8. William Shakespeare, *Hamlet*, Act III.
9. Luke 22:42.

6 Obedience

1. St Clare of Assisi, *Second Letter to Blessed Agnes of Prague*, in Armstrong and Brady, eds, *Francis and Clare: The Complete Works*, p. 196.
2. *Assisi Compilation*, I, FED 2, p. 118.
3. *Assisi Compilation*, XI, p. 125.
4. *The Principles*, Day 10.
5. Galatians 2:20.
6. W. H. Vanstone, *The Stature of Waiting*, DLT, 1982.
7. St Francis of Assisi, *Expositio in Pater Noster*, FED 1, pp. 158–9.
8. Philippians 2:8.
9. Bartholomew of Pisa, in Marion A. Habig OFM, ed., *Omnibus of Sources*, Franciscan Press, 1991, p. 1847.
10. Life of Brother Juniper, chapter 1, in *The Little Flowers of Saint Francis*, trans. Raphael Brown, Garden City, NY, Image Books (Doubleday), 1958.
11. Antony Sutch OSB, *The Tablet*, London, 2 August 2002.

Part Three: Joy

7 Living with Difference

1. 1 Cel. XXIX.
2. *The Little Flowers of Saint Francis*, chapter 8.
3. John 8:11.
4. *The Principles*, Day 12.
5. 1 Cel. XXIX.
6. St Francis of Assisi, *Letter to Brother Anthony of Padua*, FED 1, p. 107.
7. J. Hoeberichts, *Francis and Islam*, Franciscan Press, 1997.
8. 2 Cel. IV.
9. The *Earlier Rule*, chapter XIX (FED 1, p. 77) and the *Rule of 1223*, chapters I and II (FED 1, p. 100).

8 *Mirror of Perfection*

1. St Clare of Assisi, *Third Letter to Blessed Agnes of Prague*, in Armstrong and Brady, eds, *Francis and Clare: The Complete Works*, p. 200.
2. E.g. in Marco Bartoli, *Clare of Assisi*, trans. Frances Teresa OSC, DLT, 1993.
3. *Legend of St. Clare*, 1, in Regis J. Armstrong et al., eds, *Clare of Assisi: Early Documents*, New York, Franciscan Institute Publications, 1993, p. 253 (referred to hereafter as CED).
4. CED, p. 253.
5. *The Principles*, Day 5.
6. Luke 2:32.
7. *Rule of St. Clare*, 1, 3 (CED, p. 64) and *Testament of St. Clare*, 37 (CED, p. 58).
8. St Francis of Assisi, *The Form of Life Given to Clare and her Sisters*, in CED, p. 311.
9. *Rule of St. Clare*, Prologue, CED, p. 63.
10. *Legend of St. Clare*, 21–2, CED, p. 276.
11. E.g. in the appropriate allocation of food, clothes and shoes; see *Rule of St. Clare*, 3, CED, pp. 67–8.

9 *Faith in the Real World*

1. 2 Cel. CCCLXXXVI.
2. H. A. Williams, *Poverty, Chastity and Obedience*, Mitchell Beazley, 1975, p. 40.
3. *The Principles*, Day 28.
4. *The Principles*, Day 29.

Bibliography and Further Reading

(Place of publication London unless otherwise stated)

Armstrong, Regis J. and Brady, Ignatius C., eds., *Francis and Clare: The Complete Works,* Mahwah, NJ, Paulist Press, 1982

Armstrong, Regis J., Hellmann, J. A. Wayne and Short, William J., eds, *Francis of Assisi: Early Documents,* New York, New City Press:

Vol. 1: *The Saint,* 1999

Vol. 2: *The Founder,* 2000

Vol. 3: *The Prophet,* 2001

Armstrong, Regis J. et al., eds, *Clare of Assisi: Early Documents,* New York, Franciscan Institute Publications, 1993

Austin SSF, Nicholas Alan SSF and Tristam SSF, eds, *A Sense of the Divine: a Franciscan Reader for the Christian Year,* Norwich, Canterbury Press, 2001

Bartoli, Marco, *Clare of Assisi,* DLT, 1993

Brown, Raphael, trans., *The Little Flowers of Saint Francis,* Garden City, NY, Image Books (Doubleday), 1958

The Daily Office SSF, Norwich, Canterbury Press, 1992

Frances Teresa OSC, *Living the Incarnation,* DLT, 1993

Frances Teresa OSC, *This Living Mirror,* DLT, 1995

Habig, Marion A., *Omnibus of Sources,* Franciscan Press, 1991

Helen Julian CSF, *Living the Gospel,* BRF, 2001

Hoeberichts, J., *Francis and Islam,* Franciscan Press, 1997

The Principles of the First Order of the Society of Saint Francis, revised edition, 1996

Ramon SSF, *Franciscan Spirituality: Following Francis Today*, SPCK, 1994

Rinser, Luise, *Bruder Feuer*, Stuttgart, K. Thienemann, 1975

Williams, Rowan, *Writing in the Dust*, Hodder & Stoughton, 2002